BOOK OF

HOW THINGS WORK

Design: David West Children's
Book Design
Consultant: Ian Graham

The publishers would like to thank
the following artists for contributing
to this book:

Peter Bull pp. 8–11, 12–21, 26–29,
34–37, 42–51, 78–89; Neil Bullpit
pp. 38–41, 64–73; Peter Gregory
pp. 38, 52, 56, 60, 64, 70; Ian Moores
pp. 30–33, 52–63, 70–77; Rob Shone
p. 9, 12, 18, 22, 26, 30, 34, 42, 45, 48,
78, 82, 86

KINGFISHER
An imprint of Larousse plc
Elsley House
24–30 Great Titchfield Street
London W1P 7AD

This paperback edition published by Kingfisher 1995

10 9 8 7 6 5 4 3 2 1

First published by Kingfisher 1990

A CIP catalogue record for this book is available
from the British Library

ISBN 1-85697-297-6

Phototypeset by Southern Positives and Negatives (SPAN),
Lingfield, Surrey
Printed in Hong Kong

BOOK OF
HOW
THINGS
WORK

STEVE PARKER

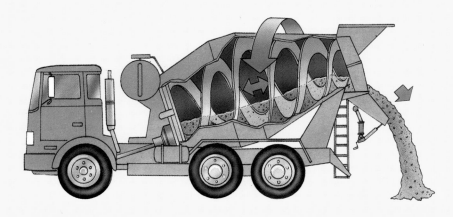

Kingfisher

CONTENTS

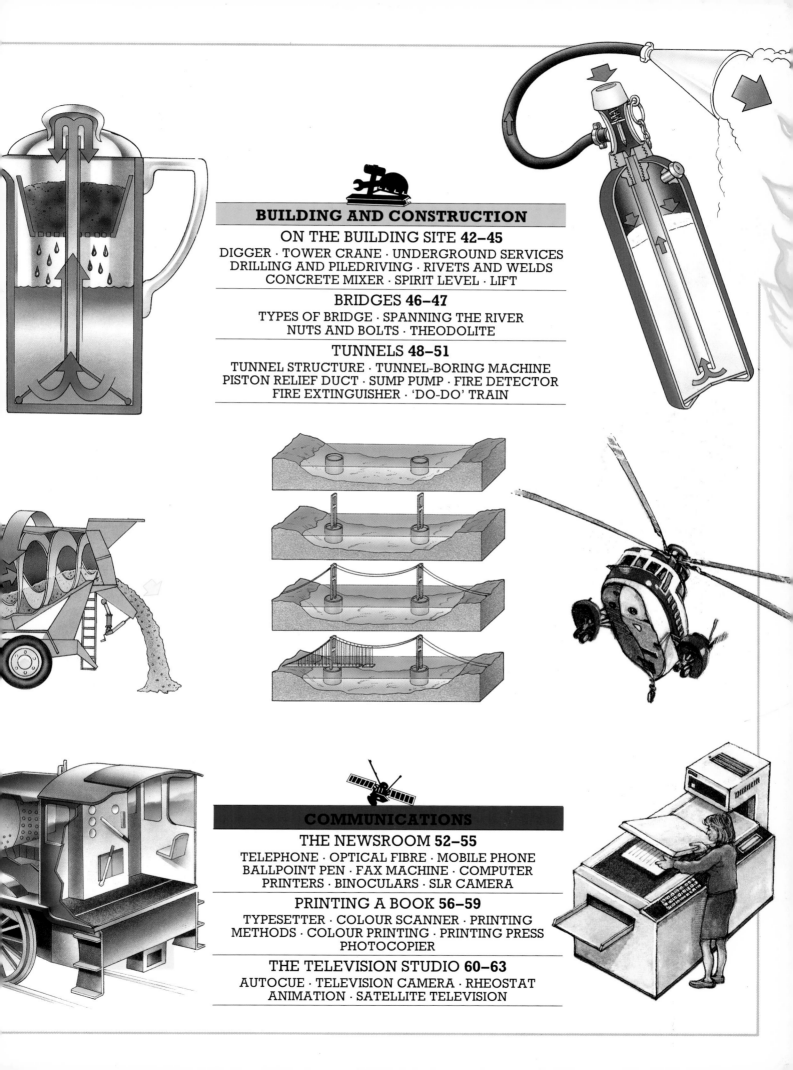

INTRODUCTION

Look around you. Unless you are reading this book on a desert island, or deep in the jungle, you should be able to see at least one kind of machine. It might be quite a simple device, such as a pair of scissors, or a nut and bolt. Or it could be a complicated one, like a music hi-fi system, a motor car, or a jumbo jet flying overhead.

How does it work? Nearly all of us have an in-built curiosity about how things work – and especially about the workings of machines and bits of equipment designed by other humans. What happens inside the shiny white box of a dishwasher? Or in the great construction machines on a building site? Or even in an electric light bulb, when you flick on the switch?

How Things Work takes the lid off dozens of machines, devices, instruments and pieces of equipment. Clear diagrams show how the parts move, and what goes where. It shows that many machines rely on basic mechanical and electrical parts, such as levers, screws, springs and electromagnets. The trick is putting these simple parts together in the right way to do the job.

The book is divided into six main sections, each based on a different aspect of our daily lives. See what happens when you wash your clothes, or turn on the lawn sprinkler in *The Home*. Find out how motorways are made and how hovercrafts ride the waves in *On the Move*. And see how news is broadcast, books are printed and television programmes are recorded in *Communications*.

Many small devices, and the principles by which they work, are used again and again in different machines. These are explained in the *Glossary*, together with less familiar terms.

So, next time you pull on a new sweater, take the train to the next town, and watch a movie – think about the many processes and machines that have gone into making these things. They have been devised and constructed by people. Someone has to invent each machine, from a humble zip, to the printing press or the Space Shuttle. Great inventors started with their in-built curiosity and a desire to make things work. Could this be you?

GETTING UP

FLUORESCENT LIGHT 6

ALARM CLOCK 1

HAIR DRIER 4

LAVATORY 5

TAP 3

AEROSOL SPRAY 8

WARMTH AND WATER 2

ZIP FASTENER 7

---

1 CLOCK

The clock is one of the most familiar machines. In an escapement-type clock (as opposed to an electric one), energy for its mechanism comes from you, as you wind it up. The escape wheel clicks round slowly like a rotating ratchet, allowing the energy from the mainspring to unwind very slowly, and by regular amounts each time. The mechanism that measures out the small bursts of movement is the *escapement mechanism*. The energy from the mainspring keeps the balance wheel swinging back and forth. The pallets alternately catch and release the escape wheel. This breaks up the irregular unwinding of the mainspring into small measured bursts of time which are then transmitted via the train of connecting gears to the minute and the hour hands.

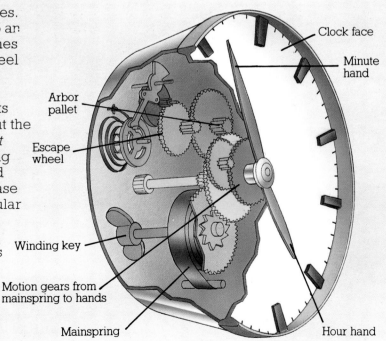

Clock face

Minute hand

Arbor pallet

Escape wheel

Winding key

Motion gears from mainspring to hands

Mainspring

Hour hand

WARMTH AND WATER

The walls and ceilings of most modern houses conceal a maze of water pipes. There are two main systems: one for the water supply itself, from taps; and a separate circuit for the central-heating system. Water from the main flows under great pressure up into the roofspace, where it fills up the cold-water tank. Usually, one pipe runs from this incoming main to the kitchen cold tap, which is why this tap has such a powerful flow if you turn it on full! Water from the cold-water tank flows to the cold taps in the bath, shower and basin, and to the lavatory (page 10).

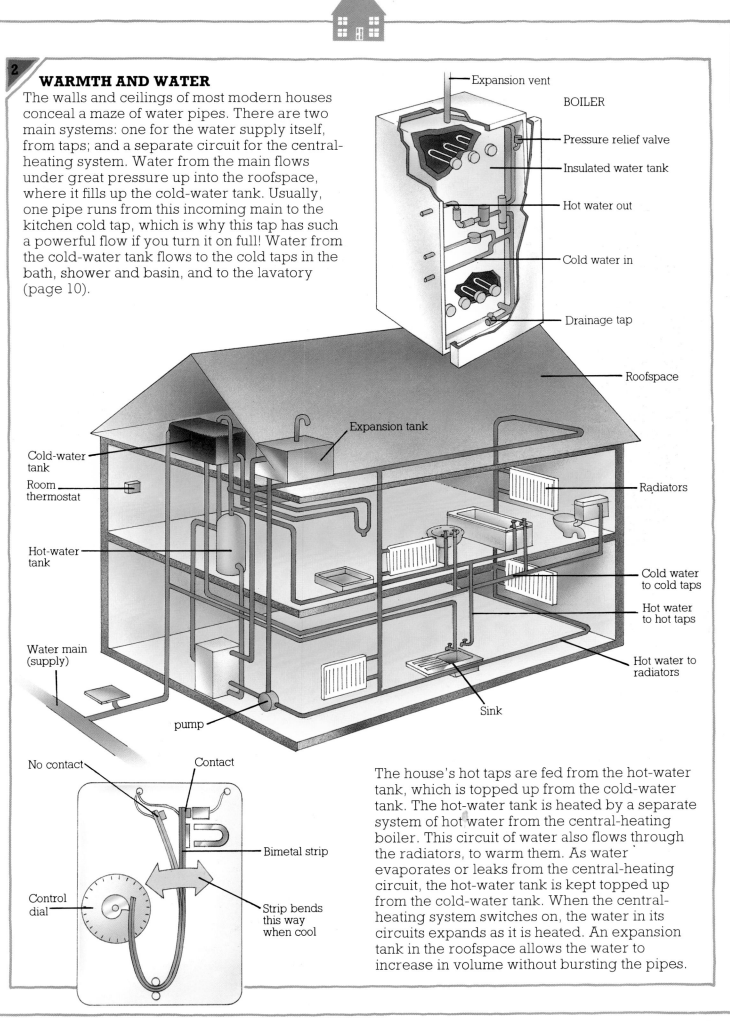

Expansion vent

BOILER

Pressure relief valve

Insulated water tank

Hot water out

Cold water in

Drainage tap

Roofspace

Expansion tank

Cold-water tank

Room thermostat

Hot-water tank

Water main (supply)

pump

Radiators

Cold water to cold taps

Hot water to hot taps

Hot water to radiators

Sink

No contact

Contact

Bimetal strip

Strip bends this way when cool

Control dial

The house's hot taps are fed from the hot-water tank, which is topped up from the cold-water tank. The hot-water tank is heated by a separate system of hot water from the central-heating boiler. This circuit of water also flows through the radiators, to warm them. As water evaporates or leaks from the central-heating circuit, the hot-water tank is kept topped up from the cold-water tank. When the central-heating system switches on, the water in its circuits expands as it is heated. An expansion tank in the roofspace allows the water to increase in volume without bursting the pipes.

3 TAP

We rarely think of what happens inside a tap, until it starts to drip. As you turn the handle, the screw mechanism inside, which presses a rubber washer onto the water pipe, lifts up. The pressure of the water trying to push through the pipe pushes the washer upwards, and so the water flows through. Water does not leak around the spindle because the spindle fits snugly inside the water-sealing nut.

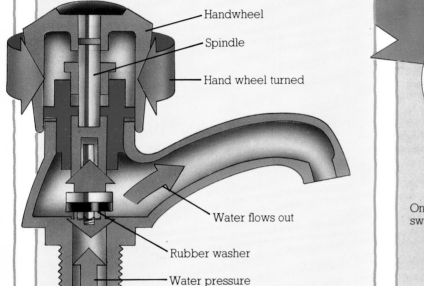

Handwheel

Spindle

Hand wheel turned

Water flows out

Rubber washer

Water pressure

4 HAIR DRIER

The drier contains a miniature electric heater to create your own warm wind. The heating element is made from special resistance wire. This partially resists the flow of electricity through it, and heat is produced as the electricity forces its way through. The fan blows moisture-laden air away from your hair, continuously replacing it with fresh, dry air.

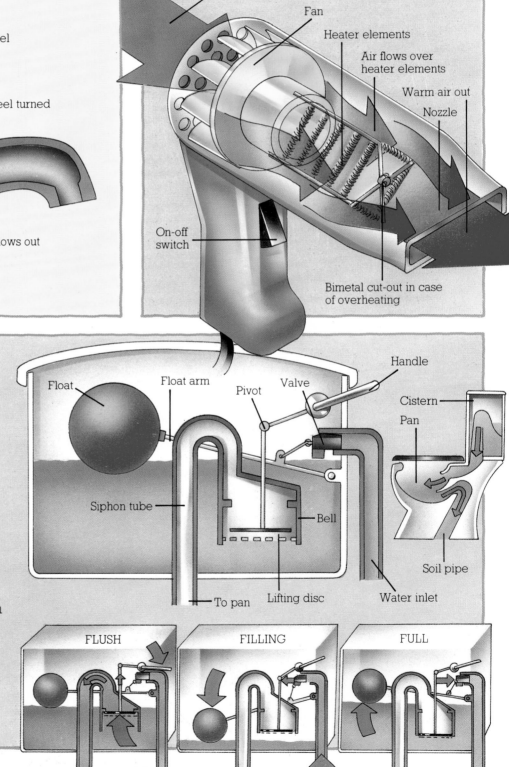

Cool air sucked in

Fan

Heater elements

Air flows over heater elements

Warm air out

Nozzle

On-off switch

Bimetal cut-out in case of overheating

5 LAVATORY

Most houses have several float valves, with one in each lavatory. As water fills the cistern, it lifts the large floating ball. Gradually the lever-arm attached to the ball closes a valve which stops the water. When you pull the handle, a large disc inside a bell lifts a quantity of water into the siphon tube. This water then falls down into the pan and 'pulls' with it the rest of the water in the cistern, by *siphonic action*. As the disc's edge wears, water leaks down past it when the handle is pulled. This is why a lavatory gradually becomes more awkward to flush.

Handle

Float

Float arm

Pivot

Valve

Cistern

Pan

Siphon tube

Bell

To pan

Lifting disc

Water inlet

Soil pipe

FLUSH

FILLING

FULL

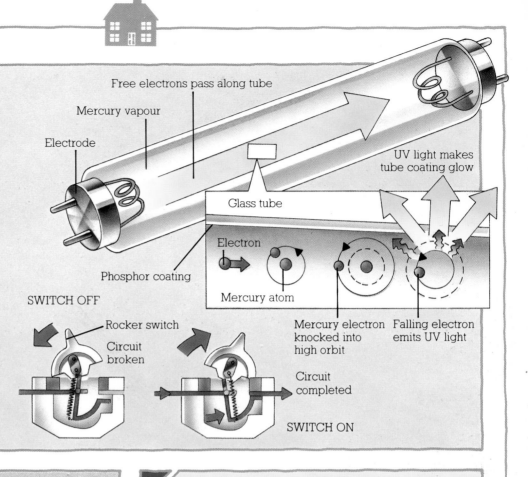

6 FLUORESCENT LIGHT

A fluorescent 'striplight' produces more light per amount of electricity than the light 'bulb' (page 84). The tube is filled with vapour of the silvery metal mercury that is found in thermometers. The metal electrode at the end of the tube gives off a beam of invisible, electrically-charged particles, called electrons. When an electron hits a mercury atom, it momentarily knocks one of the atom's own electrons out of position. When it bounces back into its correct position, it creates a burst of invisible ultraviolet energy, which is turned into visible light by the tube's internal coating.

Free electrons pass along tube

Mercury vapour

Electrode

Phosphor coating

UV light makes tube coating glow

Glass tube

Electron

Mercury atom

Mercury electron knocked into high orbit

Falling electron emits UV light

SWITCH OFF

Rocker switch

Circuit broken

Circuit completed

SWITCH ON

7 ZIP FASTENER

The zip is made of two rows of tiny teeth-and-sockets. These are opened and closed by wedges on the zip-pull. When you close the zip, the teeth come together at an angle as they slide past the upper wedge. They are then clipped together by the lower wedges, with each tooth fitting into the socket of the one in front. The first zip was invented by Whitcomb Judson in 1893.

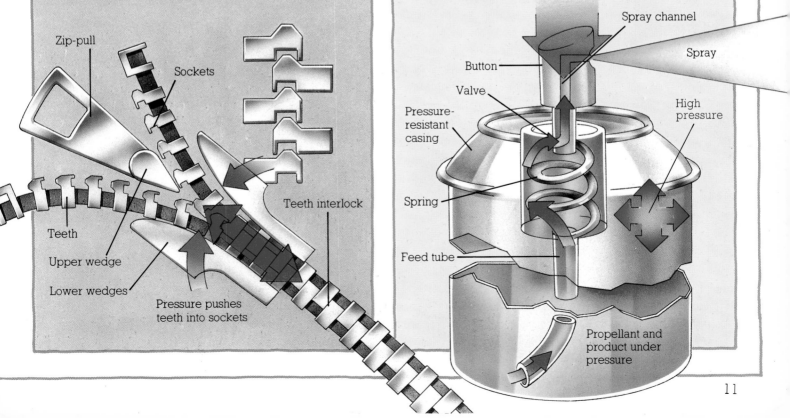

Zip-pull

Sockets

Teeth interlock

Teeth

Upper wedge

Lower wedges

Pressure pushes teeth into sockets

8 AEROSOL SPRAY

An aerosol spray can contains the product itself and the propellant that pushes it out of the can. They are under great pressure, and the outlet valve is kept closed both by this internal pressure and by a spring. As you push the button, the valve opens and allows the contents to flow. The outflow channel is very narrow and causes the product to break up into a fine, mist-like spray.

Spray channel

Spray

Button

Valve

Pressure-resistant casing

High pressure

Spring

Feed tube

Propellant and product under pressure

THE KITCHEN

MICROWAVE OVEN 9

SCALES 4

FRIDGE-FREEZER 10

ELECTRIC IRON 5

POP-UP TOASTER 2

ELECTRIC KETTLE 6

WASHING MACHINE 12

TUMBLE DRIER 13

DISHWASHER 11

COFFEE-MAKER 7

CAN-OPENER 1

WHISK 3

FOOD PROCESSOR 8

CAN-OPENER

The can-opener is a good example of the wedge. Pull down the handle, and the cutter's sharp edge acts as a gradually-widening wedge that forces its way into the lid. Turn the key, and the teeth on the wheel grip the rim and turn it around.

Handle lever

Handles pulled together to drive cutter through lid

Can

Circular cutter

Turn key

Toothed wheels turn can around

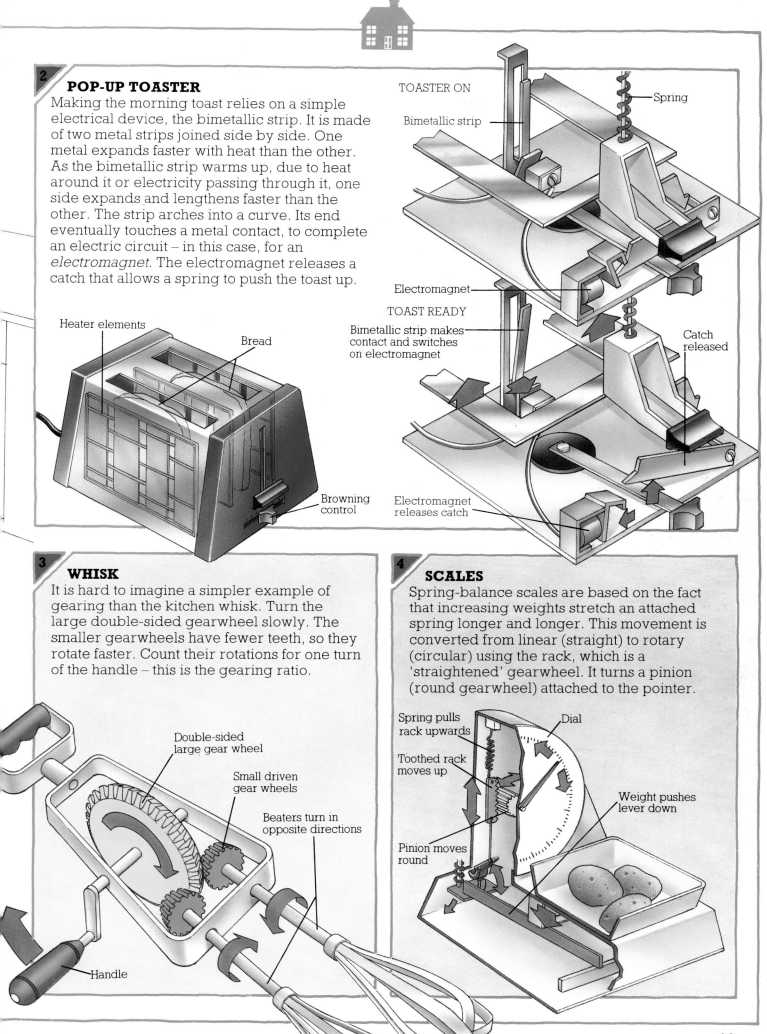

2 POP-UP TOASTER

Making the morning toast relies on a simple electrical device, the bimetallic strip. It is made of two metal strips joined side by side. One metal expands faster with heat than the other. As the bimetallic strip warms up, due to heat around it or electricity passing through it, one side expands and lengthens faster than the other. The strip arches into a curve. Its end eventually touches a metal contact, to complete an electric circuit – in this case, for an *electromagnet*. The electromagnet releases a catch that allows a spring to push the toast up.

Heater elements

Bread

Browning control

TOASTER ON

Spring

Bimetallic strip

Electromagnet

TOAST READY

Bimetallic strip makes contact and switches on electromagnet

Catch released

Electromagnet releases catch

3 WHISK

It is hard to imagine a simpler example of gearing than the kitchen whisk. Turn the large double-sided gearwheel slowly. The smaller gearwheels have fewer teeth, so they rotate faster. Count their rotations for one turn of the handle – this is the gearing ratio.

Double-sided large gear wheel

Small driven gear wheels

Beaters turn in opposite directions

Handle

4 SCALES

Spring-balance scales are based on the fact that increasing weights stretch an attached spring longer and longer. This movement is converted from linear (straight) to rotary (circular) using the rack, which is a 'straightened' gearwheel. It turns a pinion (round gearwheel) attached to the pointer.

Spring pulls rack upwards

Dial

Toothed rack moves up

Weight pushes lever down

Pinion moves round

5 ELECTRIC IRON

Old-fashioned 'smoothing irons' were warmed on a stand near the fire or hotplate. Today's electric version has its own heater element that warms the sole-plate. Most materials press more smoothly if they are damp, since moisture softens the tiny fibres in the material and makes them flexible. So the 'steam iron' sprays steam or a fine mist of hot water onto the material.

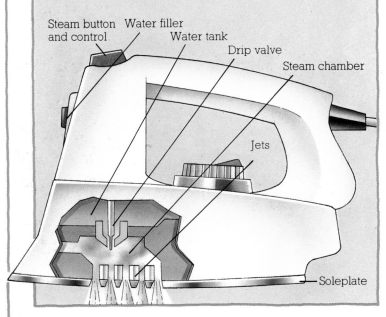

Steam button and control
Water filler
Water tank
Drip valve
Steam chamber
Jets
Soleplate

6 ELECTRIC KETTLE

Like the iron, the modern kettle has its own electrical heater element. It also contains two failsafe circuit-breakers, or cut-outs. One stops the electric current to the heater when the water reaches boiling point. The other does the same if the kettle boils dry. The mains plug and socket must be designed so that water cannot drip into them and cause a short-circuit.

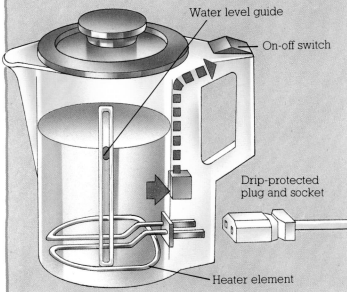

Water level guide
On-off switch
Drip-protected plug and socket
Heater element

7 COFFEE-MAKER

In a coffee-grinder, beans slide down between two ridged metal surfaces that fit closely together. The turning motion crushes the beans into a fine powder, until the pieces are small enough to fall into the tray below. The percolator uses the principle that boiling water produces bubbles of steam that rise. The bubbles rise up the central spout carrying water with them, to create a fountain at the top. The hot water percolates, or oozes, back down through the ground coffee, dissolving the coffee-flavoured substances as it goes.

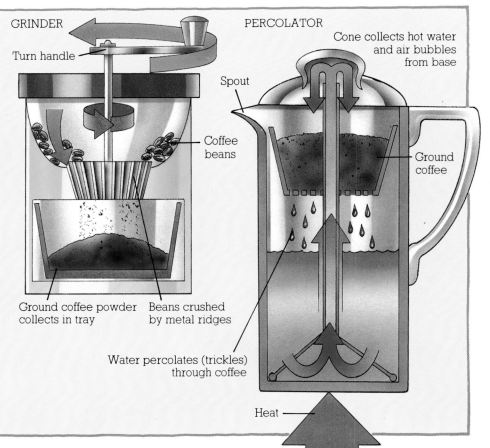

GRINDER
Turn handle
Coffee beans
Ground coffee powder collects in tray
Beans crushed by metal ridges

PERCOLATOR
Cone collects hot water and air bubbles from base
Spout
Ground coffee
Water percolates (trickles) through coffee
Heat

8 FOOD PROCESSOR

The food processor is another kitchen device that uses electrical power instead of muscle power. Inside, the typical processor is relatively simple. An electric motor turns the spindle via a flexible toothed belt. Each differently-shaped attachment does a specific job, from slicing to shredding to beating to liquidizing. Ingredients are dropped into the feed tube, or pushed in using a plunger. This keeps fingers away from the whirling blades; safe design is a vital feature of many machines.

Controls

Electric motor

Attachment slots onto splines (ridges) on spindle

Feed tube

Lid

Toothed belt

Spindle

9 MICROWAVE OVEN

Microwaves are part of the spectrum of *electromagnetic waves*, which includes light waves and X-rays. They have wavelengths from about 30 centimetres to one millimetre, which places them between the shortest radio waves and infra-red (heat) waves. One of their properties is to 'excite' molecules, especially in liquids, and make them vibrate and heat up. So foods with a large proportion of water, such as soups, cook quickest.

The waves are produced by a *magnetron*, a type of electron tube. They are scattered around the oven by a metal fan, for more even cooking. They pass through most types of china and glass, but not metals.

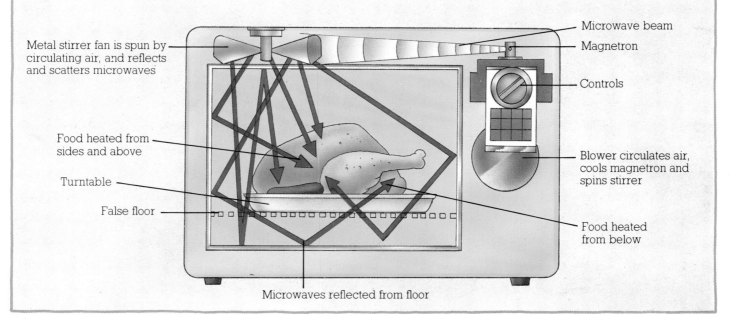

Metal stirrer fan is spun by circulating air, and reflects and scatters microwaves

Microwave beam

Magnetron

Controls

Food heated from sides and above

Turntable

False floor

Blower circulates air, cools magnetron and spins stirrer

Food heated from below

Microwaves reflected from floor

10 FRIDGE-FREEZER

A fridge-freezer works as a heat-exchanger, extracting warmth from the air inside the unit, and passing it into the air outside. The coolant is a special fluid that flows around a closed circuit inside pipes, from evaporator to condenser. In the evaporator, the coolant boils and evaporates. It draws the energy it needs to evaporate as heat from its surroundings. It then flows through a compressor which increases its pressure and pumps it to the condenser. Here it turns from a gas back into a liquid, and gives out its heat to the air as it does so. From here, it returns to the evaporator and the process starts again.

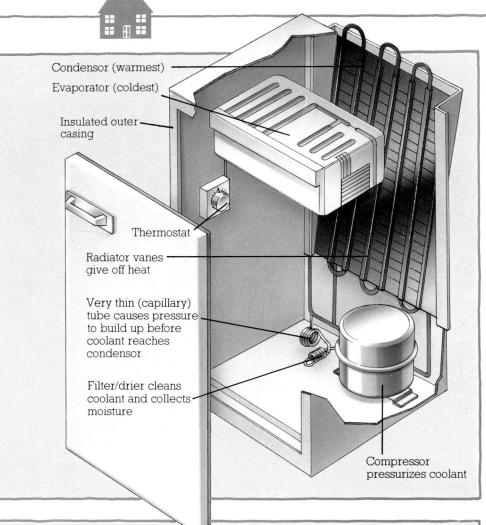

Condensor (warmest)
Evaporator (coldest)
Insulated outer casing
Thermostat
Radiator vanes give off heat
Very thin (capillary) tube causes pressure to build up before coolant reaches condensor
Filter/drier cleans coolant and collects moisture
Compressor pressurizes coolant

11 DISHWASHER

Dirty crockery and cutlery are loaded into specially designed carriers, so that the water spray can reach all parts and the water can drain away freely afterwards. The pressure of the water itself makes the jets spin around. The first part of the cycle uses water containing detergent, to dissolve grease and grime. The detergent is loaded into a compartment in the door. In the second part of the cycle, clean water rinses away the soapy water. Then a heating element warms and dries the load.

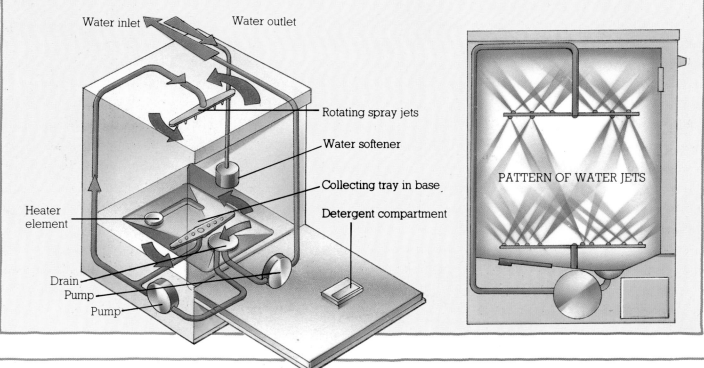

Water inlet
Water outlet
Rotating spray jets
Water softener
Collecting tray in base
Detergent compartment
Heater element
Drain
Pump
Pump
PATTERN OF WATER JETS

WASHING MACHINE

12

A modern washing machine relies on several regulatory mechanisms in its operation. At the start of the cycle, water pours in through an electrically-controlled inlet valve. Once the water reaches a certain level in the drum, this is detected by a sensor that closes the inlet valve. The pressure of the water in the inlet pipe helps to shut the valve firmly. The water is then heated by the machine's heater element. Once the pre-set temperature is reached, a *thermostat* switches off the electricity supply to the heater. A load of washing and water is very heavy, so the drum is stabilized by weights and suspended by heavy-duty springs.

Rotating drum

Water runs through detergent compartment into drum

Inlet valve

Controls

Heater element

Filter

Drain pump

Main motor

Water outlet

Suspension springs

TUMBLE DRIER

13

In most tumble driers, the electric motor is programmed to turn the drum one way, and then go into reverse and spin it the other way. This helps to shake and separate the contents. It prevents them from clumping together and leaving a still-damp patch in the middle, which the drying air cannot reach. Hot air is drawn through the unit by a blower fan. As it passes through the load, the air picks up dust and fibres; these are trapped by the filter screen. In order to heat such great volumes of air, tumble driers use lots of electricity. They have one of the highest running costs of all household machines.

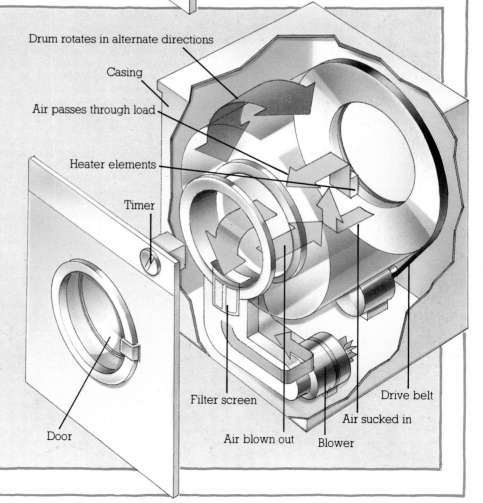

Drum rotates in alternate directions

Casing

Air passes through load

Heater elements

Timer

Filter screen

Air blown out

Blower

Air sucked in

Drive belt

Door

THE GARDEN

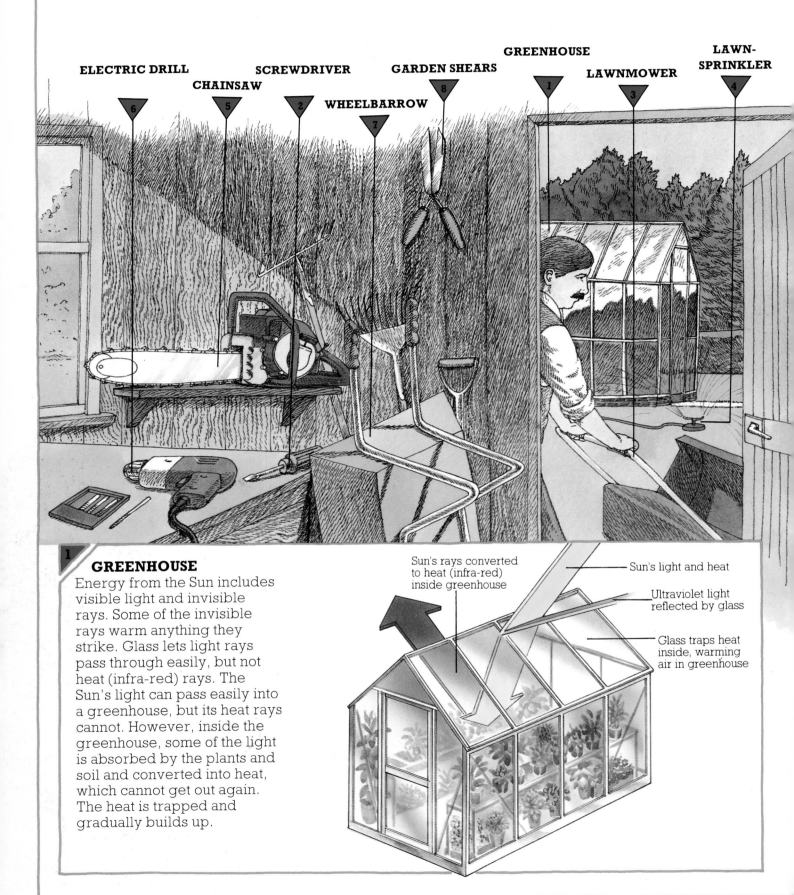

ELECTRIC DRILL 6

CHAINSAW 5

SCREWDRIVER 2

WHEELBARROW 7

GARDEN SHEARS 8

GREENHOUSE 1

LAWNMOWER 3

LAWN-SPRINKLER 4

1 GREENHOUSE

Energy from the Sun includes visible light and invisible rays. Some of the invisible rays warm anything they strike. Glass lets light rays pass through easily, but not heat (infra-red) rays. The Sun's light can pass easily into a greenhouse, but its heat rays cannot. However, inside the greenhouse, some of the light is absorbed by the plants and soil and converted into heat, which cannot get out again. The heat is trapped and gradually builds up.

Sun's rays converted to heat (infra-red) inside greenhouse

Sun's light and heat

Ultraviolet light reflected by glass

Glass traps heat inside, warming air in greenhouse

2 SCREWDRIVER

This acts like a kind of lever. Your hand moves in a large circle as you turn the handle. The turning force, or torque, is transmitted down the shaft and blade, into the screw head's slot. The screw turns in a smaller circle, but with greater turning power. Slot-headed screws are for general work. Cross-headed screws are less likely to let the blade slip out and damage the nearby surface.

Small force turning large distance

Handle

Shaft

Head

Large force turning small distance

Screw acts as spiral ramp

3 LAWNMOWER

Like the screwdriver, the lawnmower is a rotary machine. In the hand-pushed type, the heavy back roller is linked to the rotating blades by a chain. The rotating blades are angled in the form of a shallow helix, so that each one approaches the base blade with a scissor-like action. Grass is trapped between the two, snipped off, and thrown into the grass box.

The height of the cut is adjusted by lowering or raising the small front roller. In a powered mower, a small petrol engine or electric motor drives the back roller and blades.

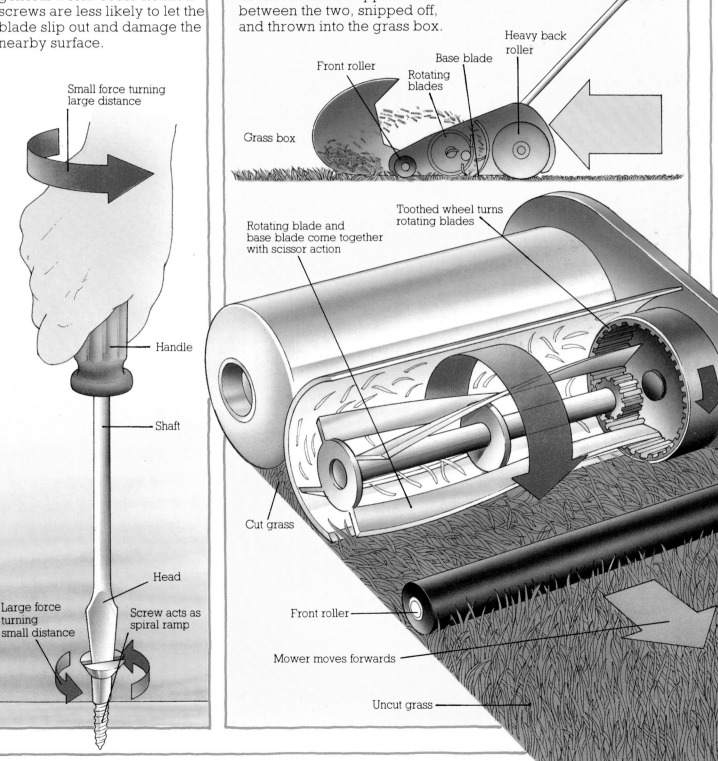

Handle

Heavy back roller

Base blade

Rotating blades

Front roller

Grass box

Rotating blade and base blade come together with scissor action

Toothed wheel turns rotating blades

Cut grass

Front roller

Mower moves forwards

Uncut grass

4 LAWN-SPRINKLER

The oscillating sprinkler is based on the principle of the water wheel. The pressure of the water coming through the hosepipe turns a small fan-shaped water wheel. A series of gears slows down the spinning speed, and a crank fixed to a rotating wheel changes the circular motion to an oscillating one (swinging to and fro like a pendulum). By changing the length of the crank, the sprayer can be made to cover a wide or narrow area on either side.

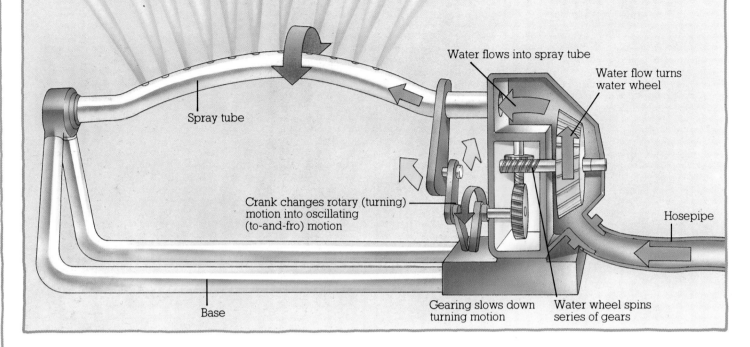

Spray tube

Water flows into spray tube

Water flow turns water wheel

Crank changes rotary (turning) motion into oscillating (to-and-fro) motion

Hosepipe

Base

Gearing slows down turning motion

Water wheel spins series of gears

5 CHAINSAW

In a hand saw, the teeth oscillate (move to and fro). The chainsaw has a 'never-ending' blade, in the shape of a chain loop bearing teeth. A small engine, usually petrol-driven, turns the drive cog and makes the chain move around its loop. The chain soon becomes hot and tends to stick in its guides, so oil is regularly dripped onto it from a small tank, for cooling and lubrication. Safety is vital. Users wear strong gloves, protective goggles, shin-guards and thick boots, in case the cutting chain slips and falls.

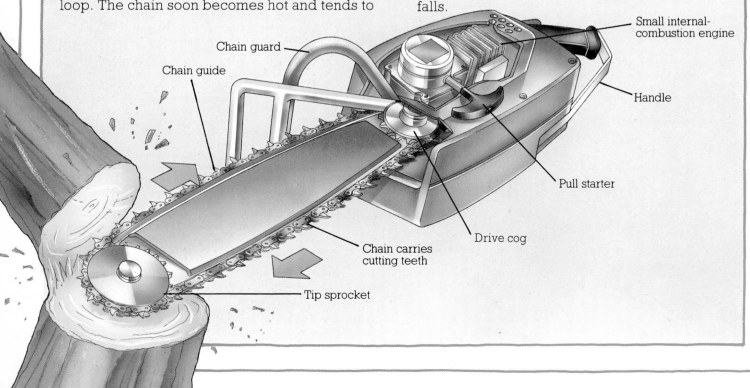

Chain guard

Chain guide

Small internal-combustion engine

Handle

Pull starter

Drive cog

Chain carries cutting teeth

Tip sprocket

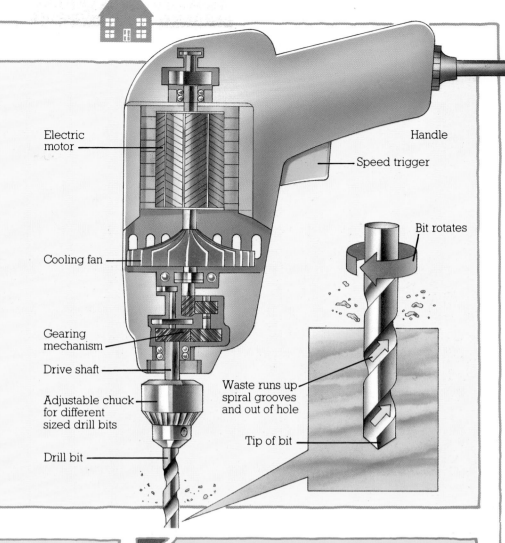

6 · ELECTRIC DRILL

The small electric motor in a drill is extremely powerful, and its turning force is increased as it is slowed down by the gearing mechanism. Many drills have adjustable speeds, either by varying the electrical voltage fed to the motor, or by changing the gears in the gear train (page 58). Speeds of only a few hundred rpm (revolutions per minute) are suitable for tough materials such as concrete and hard metal. Several thousand rpm can be used in softer materials such as softwoods and plastics.

Electric motor

Handle

Speed trigger

Cooling fan

Gearing mechanism

Drive shaft

Adjustable chuck for different sized drill bits

Drill bit

Bit rotates

Waste runs up spiral grooves and out of hole

Tip of bit

7 · WHEELBARROW

The wheelbarrow is one of the simplest examples of a lever. The pivot point, or fulcrum, is at one end, the load is in the middle and the effort is applied to the other end. Using a wheelbarrow, you can lift a large weight over a small distance, by applying your small lifting effort over a large distance.

Effort moves greater distance

Fulcrum at wheel

Load moves small distance

8 · GARDEN SHEARS

Two levers connected together give the shears plenty of cutting power. Shearing pressure is greatest near the fulcrum. The blades should be sharp and come together without gaps or twisting.

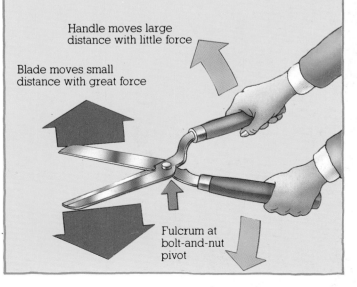

Handle moves large distance with little force

Blade moves small distance with great force

Fulcrum at bolt-and-nut pivot

THE STREET

PADLOCK 5

PUMPS AND VALVES 4

SKIP LORRY 8

TRAFFIC SIGNALS 7

COMBINATION LOCK 6

BRAKES 3

GEARS 2

BALANCING 1

ROAD DRILL 9

1 BALANCING

A spinning wheel acts as a simple gyroscope (page 39). It resists attempts to change position. Hold a rotating wheel as shown, and feel the resistance as you try to tip it. This *gyroscopic inertia* helps you to balance on a bicycle.

2 GEARS

Pedalling downhill, the chain runs from the large front sprocket to the small rear one. For every turn of the pedals, the road wheel turns many times, but with limited turning force. Uphill, the chain runs from the small front

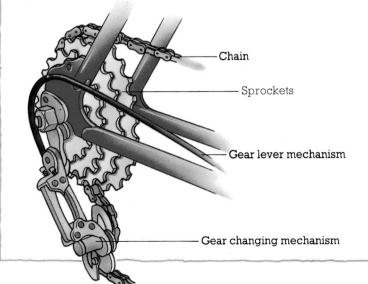

Chain

Sprockets

Gear lever mechanism

Gear changing mechanism

BRAKES

Brakes do not press on the bicycle tyre – they would soon wear a hole in it! They press on the wheel rim. The two metal arms, or yokes, work as levers. They close the blocks onto the rim with a scissor action, for even pressure on each side. Use the rear brake for routine braking, and both brakes in an emergency. Do not pull hard on the front brake alone. You could fly over the handlebars.

BRAKES OFF **BRAKES ON**

Cable

Yokes Pivot

Spring

Brake shoes

Tyre

PUMPS AND VALVES

These are components of many machines, from taps to jet planes. The pump applies pressure to a fluid (gas or liquid), for example, by a piston (page 69). This makes the fluid flow to a region of lower pressure. Non-return valve designs are many and varied, but their main job is to allow fluid to flow one way but not the other. Some valves use hinged 'doors', others have flexible diaphragms or lever-operated closures.

Handle

Plunger

Valve

VALVE OPEN VALVE CLOSED

Hose

Inner tube

Valve

Tyre

AIR IN AIR OUT

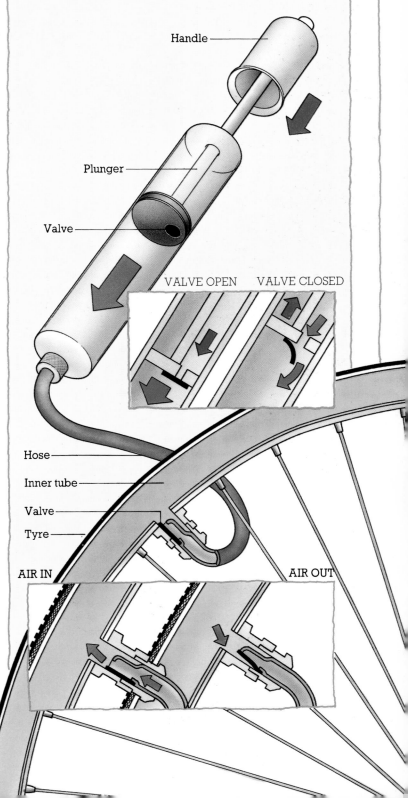

sprocket to the large rear one. The road wheel turns more slowly but with greater force. Racing cyclists use gears to keep up their natural rate of pedalling whether going uphill or down.

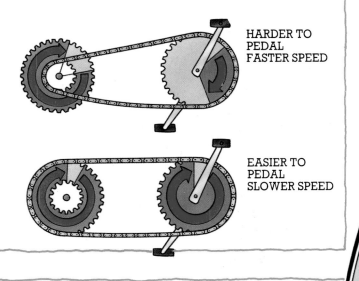

HARDER TO PEDAL FASTER SPEED

EASIER TO PEDAL SLOWER SPEED

5 PADLOCK

This small security device has the same basic mechanism as a door lock or a car ignition. Grooves and ridges run lengthwise along the key, and the keyhole is shaped to accept only keys of a certain shape. When inserted, the key's V-cuts push small locking pins into exact alignment (a straight line), which permits the locking cylinder (barrel) to turn. A lever at its end drags back the locking bolt, thereby freeing the lock.

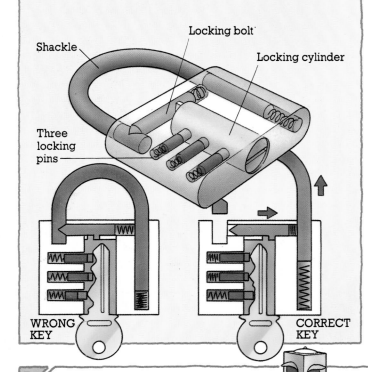

Shackle

Locking bolt

Locking cylinder

Three locking pins

WRONG KEY

CORRECT KEY

6 COMBINATION LOCK

Like the padlock, the combination lock relies on alignment. In this case, only when the tumblers are turned to the correct number combination, do the slots inside them line up. This lets you withdraw the key. With four number tumblers, and the numbers 0–9 on each one, how many possible number combinations are there?

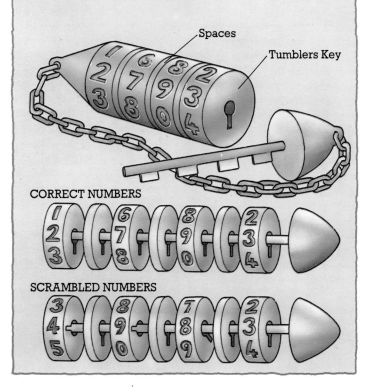

Spaces

Tumblers Key

CORRECT NUMBERS

SCRAMBLED NUMBERS

7 TRAFFIC SIGNALS

Older-type signals run to a pre-set timed cycle. If a car pulls up just as they change from green to red, it has to wait for the cycle to be completed before the lights will change to green again. Newer-style signals respond to a car's presence. The car's metal parts interfere with a weak magnetic field set up by the electrical wire buried in the road. The control box senses this and, if there are no cars waiting to move in the other directions, it switches the signals to green.

Signal

CAR INTERFERES WITH MAGNETIC FIELD

Control box

Magnetic field

Loop in road

8 SKIP LORRY

A skip lorry has a powerful hydraulic system enabling it to lift heavy loads. The power for the system is taken from the lorry's diesel engine via gearing and a control box. A hydraulic ram pushes the lifting arm; this is the effort moving the lever. The load is the skip, which moves in an arc as it is unloaded or loaded. If the tipping hooks are raised, they snag, or catch the base of the skip – and the skip truck becomes a tip-truck.

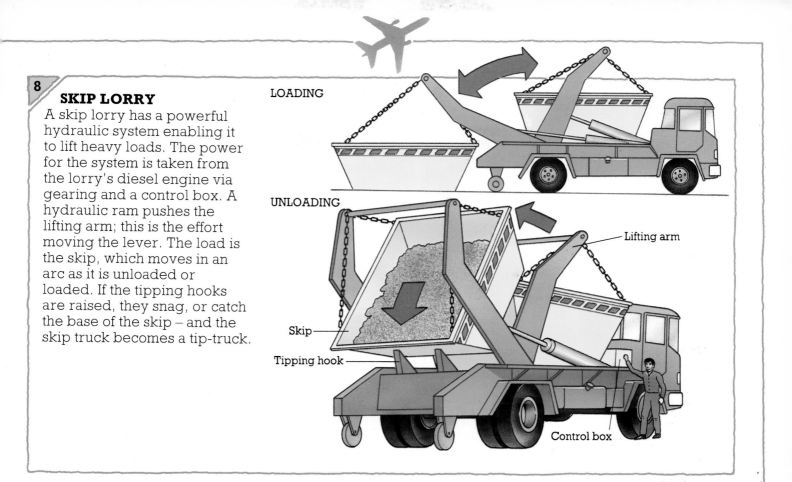

LOADING

UNLOADING

Lifting arm

Skip

Tipping hook

Control box

9 ROAD DRILL

Unlike the rotary electric drill (page 21), the road drill is pneumatic and percussive. 'Pneumatic' means that it is driven by compressed air (page 30). This is important for safety, since it means there are no trailing electrical wires. 'Percussive' refers to hitting. The drill breaks into the road surface using a fast series of hammer-blows. These are produced by a flip-flop diaphragm valve which re-routes the air many times each second, alternately raising and lowering the piston.

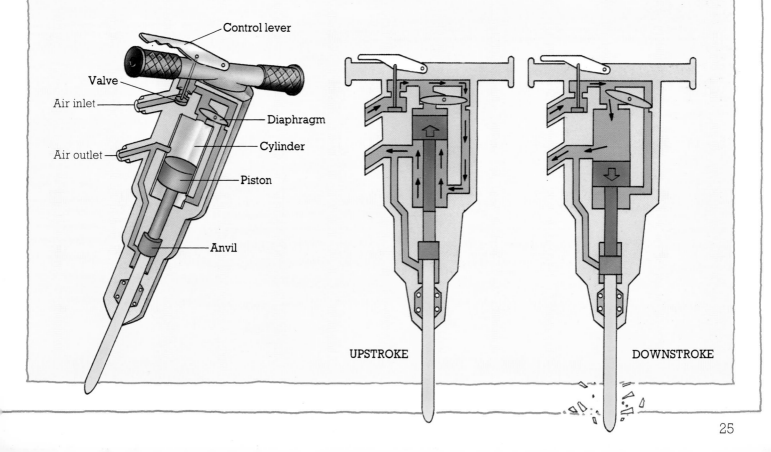

Control lever

Valve

Air inlet

Air outlet

Diaphragm

Cylinder

Piston

Anvil

UPSTROKE

DOWNSTROKE

TAKING TO THE TRACKS

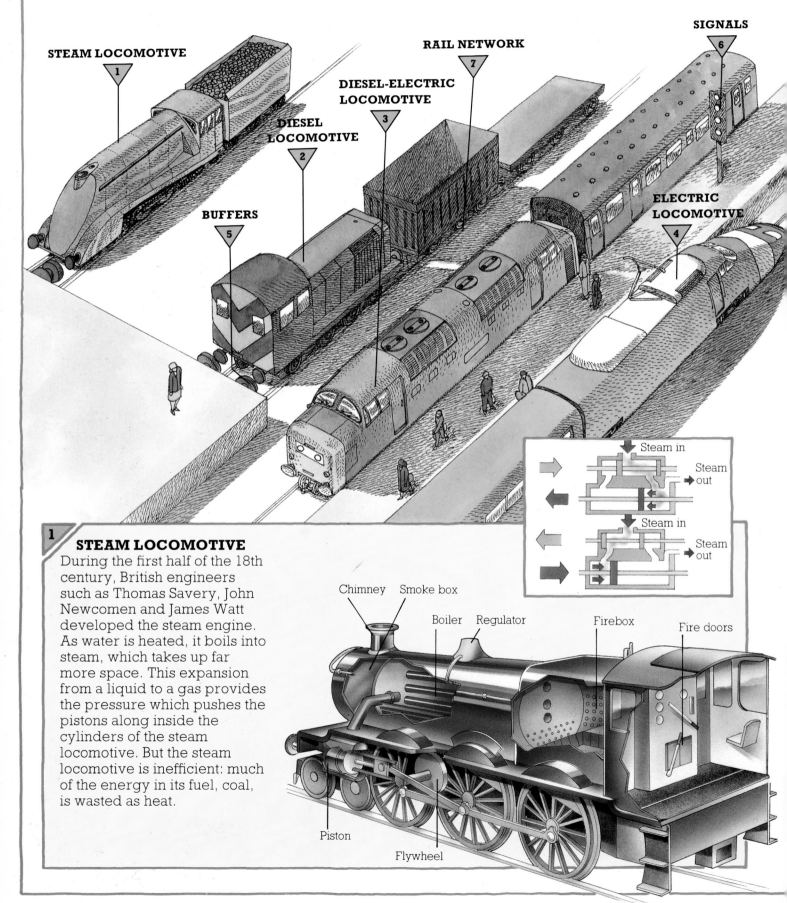

STEAM LOCOMOTIVE 1

DIESEL LOCOMOTIVE 2

DIESEL-ELECTRIC LOCOMOTIVE 3

RAIL NETWORK 7

SIGNALS 6

BUFFERS 5

ELECTRIC LOCOMOTIVE 4

Steam in

Steam out

Steam in

Steam out

1 **STEAM LOCOMOTIVE**
During the first half of the 18th century, British engineers such as Thomas Savery, John Newcomen and James Watt developed the steam engine. As water is heated, it boils into steam, which takes up far more space. This expansion from a liquid to a gas provides the pressure which pushes the pistons along inside the cylinders of the steam locomotive. But the steam locomotive is inefficient: much of the energy in its fuel, coal, is wasted as heat.

Chimney   Smoke box

Boiler   Regulator

Firebox

Fire doors

Piston

Flywheel

2 DIESEL LOCOMOTIVE

The sources of power for this locomotive are diesel engines (page 67). The diesel engine was invented in the 1890s by the French-born German engineer Rudolf Diesel. Diesel engines are more efficient than steam ones: their fuel contains more energy per weight than coal, and their maintenance time and running costs are lower. Immense force is transmitted to the driving wheel through a hydraulic gearing system. The most powerful steam locomotives, American 'Big Boys', produced 7000 horsepower (about 5.25 million watts). Diesel locomotives are capable of similar feats.

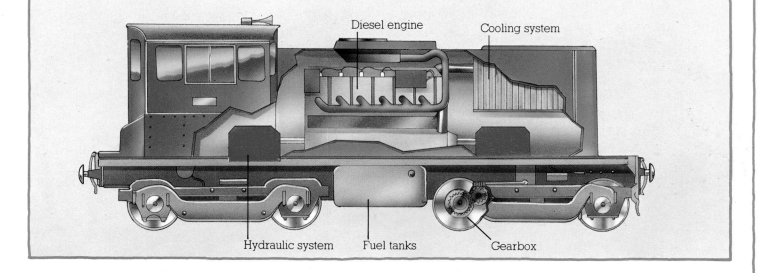

Diesel engine

Cooling system

Hydraulic system

Fuel tanks

Gearbox

3 DIESEL-ELECTRIC LOCOMOTIVE

This traction (pulling) unit is in effect an electric locomotive with its own source of electricity. The diesel engine turns a large generator, which produces electricity to drive electric motors. There is usually one electric motor on each axle. The motors are efficient and flexible, since they produce high turning force even at low speeds. This means that there is no need for an expensive and energy-wasting gear system. Union Pacific Railroad's turbo-charged diesel-electric locomotives are the most powerful, producing 6600 horsepower (about 4.95 million watts).

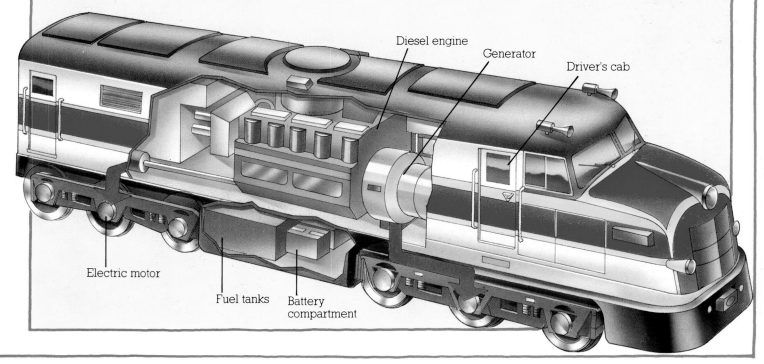

Diesel engine

Generator

Driver's cab

Electric motor

Fuel tanks

Battery compartment

4 ELECTRIC LOCOMOTIVE

The electric locomotive picks up electricity at 25,000 volts AC (alternating current) from overhead, or trackside, power lines. This is converted into DC (direct current) by *rectifiers* and reduced to the lower voltage by *transformers*, and fed via motor control circuits to the drive motors. These are mounted in the locomotive, or 'power car', and they drive the wheels through a series of gears. The main disadvantage of this system is the high cost of building and maintaining the overhead power lines.

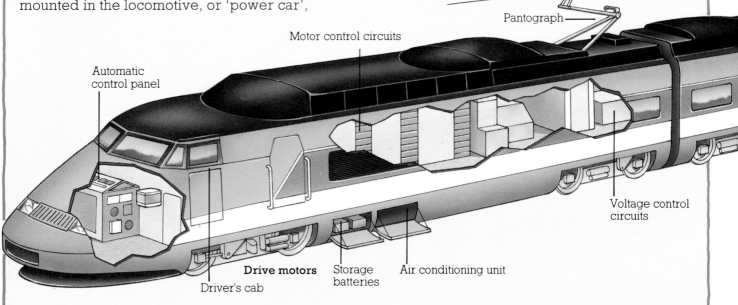

High voltage overhead power lines

Pantograph

Motor control circuits

Automatic control panel

Voltage control circuits

Drive motors
Driver's cab
Storage batteries
Air conditioning unit

5 BUFFERS

Stationary buffers are mounted at the end of a railway line. Buffers are also fitted to locomotives, passenger carriages and freight wagons. The metal spring and hydraulic damping fluid absorb the energy of the moving vehicle, causing it to slow down gradually without shocks or jarring.

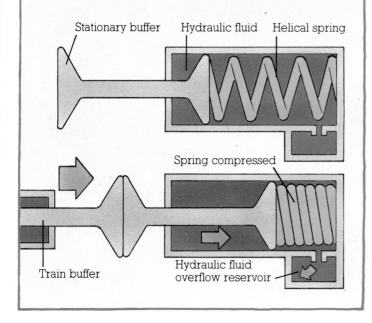

Stationary buffer   Hydraulic fluid   Helical spring

Spring compressed

Train buffer

Hydraulic fluid overflow reservoir

6 SIGNALS

Each rail network has its own signal design. The basic function of the signals is to inform the train driver that the line is clear, or to warn that it is not. The four-aspect system gives plenty of time for the driver to slow the train, so that passengers are not jerked by a sudden halt.

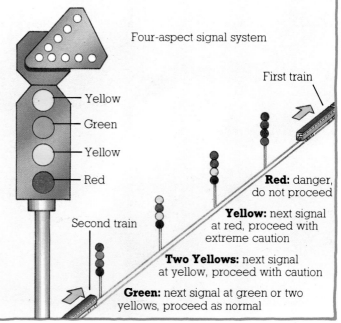

Four-aspect signal system

First train

Yellow
Green
Yellow
Red

Second train

Red: danger, do not proceed

Yellow: next signal at red, proceed with extreme caution

Two Yellows: next signal at yellow, proceed with caution

Green: next signal at green or two yellows, proceed as normal

RAIL NETWORK

Today's railway system is a complicated maze of tracks, points, signals, crossings, passenger stations and freight yards. Most trains cannot climb steep gradients, so the tracks have to be made relatively level, by building cuttings through hills and embankments in valleys. The main signal boxes are the 'nerve centres' of the network, controlling the signals and the points. They can divert a slower goods train to allow through a passenger express, or switch a commuter train onto a local line for suburban stations.

There are approximately 555,000 kilometres of track in North America, 90,000 in South America, 420,000 in Europe, 145,000 in Asia, and 75,000 in Africa. The world's longest railway line runs across Russia from Moscow to the east coast, a distance of almost 9500 kilometres with a journey time of more than eight days.

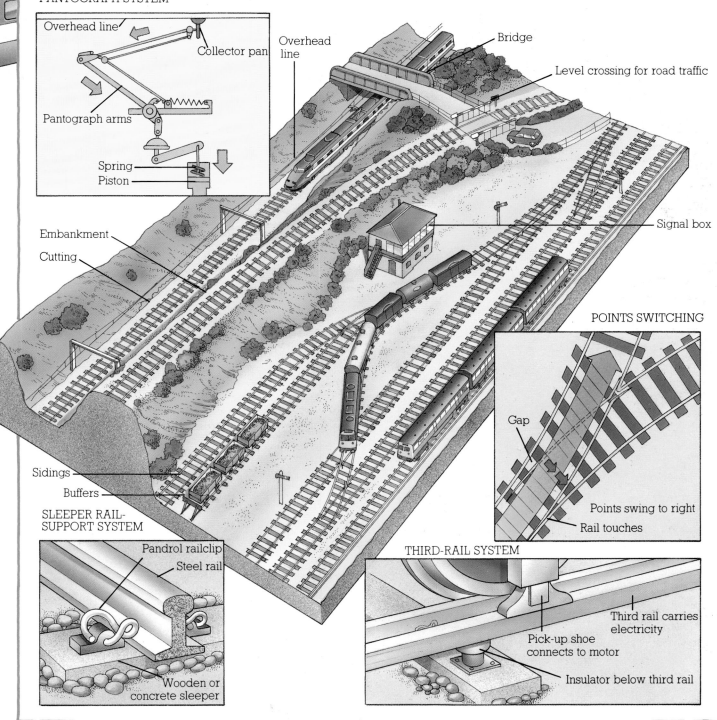

PANTOGRAPH SYSTEM
Overhead line
Collector pan
Pantograph arms
Spring
Piston

Overhead line

Bridge

Level crossing for road traffic

Signal box

Embankment

Cutting

POINTS SWITCHING

Gap

Points swing to right
Rail touches

Sidings

Buffers

SLEEPER RAIL-SUPPORT SYSTEM
Pandrol railclip
Steel rail
Wooden or concrete sleeper

THIRD-RAIL SYSTEM
Third rail carries electricity
Pick-up shoe connects to motor
Insulator below third rail

THE MOTORWAY

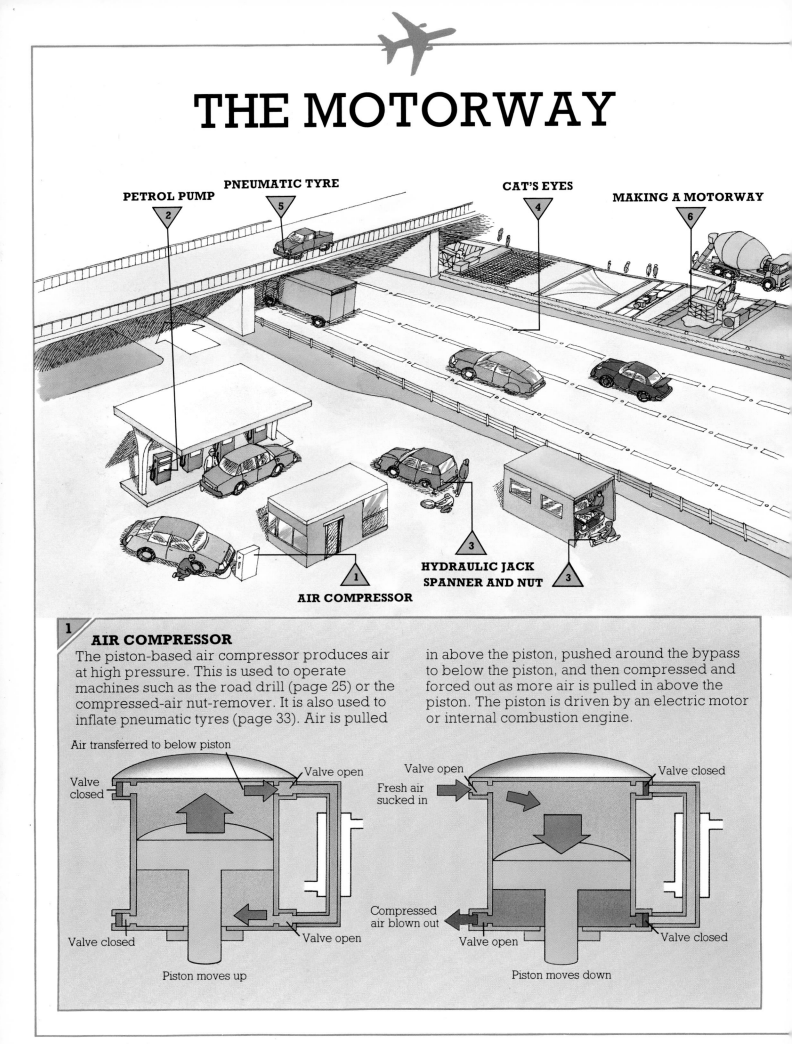

PETROL PUMP 2

PNEUMATIC TYRE 5

CAT'S EYES 4

MAKING A MOTORWAY 6

1

AIR COMPRESSOR

3 **HYDRAULIC JACK SPANNER AND NUT** 3

1 AIR COMPRESSOR

The piston-based air compressor produces air at high pressure. This is used to operate machines such as the road drill (page 25) or the compressed-air nut-remover. It is also used to inflate pneumatic tyres (page 33). Air is pulled in above the piston, pushed around the bypass to below the piston, and then compressed and forced out as more air is pulled in above the piston. The piston is driven by an electric motor or internal combustion engine.

Air transferred to below piston

Valve open

Valve closed

Valve closed

Valve open

Piston moves up

Valve open

Fresh air sucked in

Valve closed

Valve open

Compressed air blown out

Valve closed

Piston moves down

2 PETROL PUMP

There are several main mechanisms within a petrol pump. One is the motor-driven pump itself, which draws up fuel from the large underground storage tank. Next is the filter to remove dirt and impurities, and the air separator which draws off bubbles of air and other gases. Then comes the meter that measures the volume, or quantity, of fuel passing through, and shows the amount on the dial or display. Finally, there is the hose and nozzle. There is often a detector in the hose, warning that the fuel tank of the vehicle is becoming full.

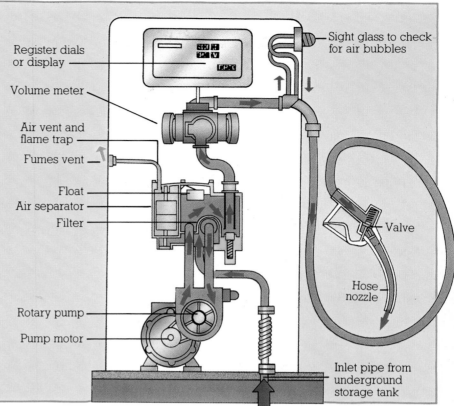

Register dials or display
Volume meter
Air vent and flame trap
Fumes vent
Float
Air separator
Filter
Rotary pump
Pump motor
Sight glass to check for air bubbles
Valve
Hose nozzle
Inlet pipe from underground storage tank

3 HYDRAULIC JACK

The vehicle jack converts a small force pushing a long way, into a large force pushing a short way. The jack's handle pushes a small piston a long way. This creates pressure in the hydraulic fluid, which presses on a secondary, or slave, piston. The slave piston has a much larger area, so it moves a short way but with greater total force. When the handle is pumped repeatedly, the jack gradually rises.

SPANNER AND NUT

The spanner's action is based on the lever principle: a small force moving a greater distance is converted into a greater force moving a small distance. The flat sides on the nut should fit snugly inside the corresponding slots in a spanner.

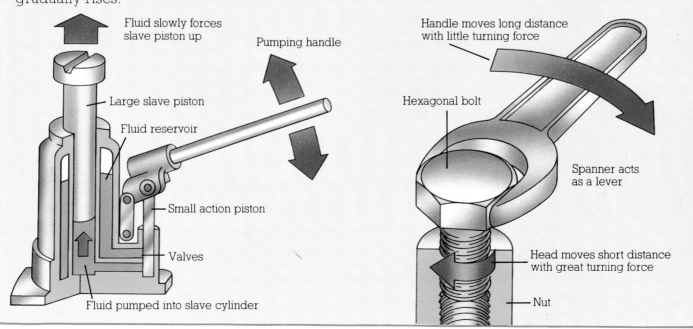

Fluid slowly forces slave piston up
Pumping handle
Large slave piston
Fluid reservoir
Small action piston
Valves
Fluid pumped into slave cylinder

Handle moves long distance with little turning force
Hexagonal bolt
Spanner acts as a lever
Head moves short distance with great turning force
Nut

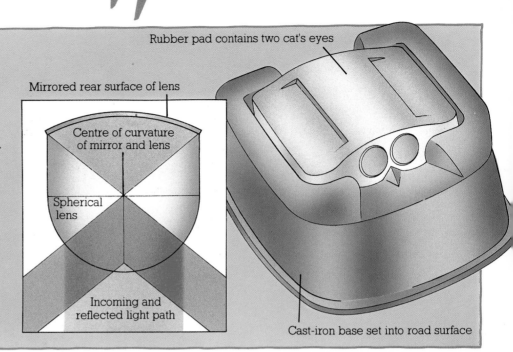

4 CAT'S EYES

Driving in the dark would be much more difficult without road reflectors to define the lane markings. The reflector contains a curved mirror and a half-spherical lens (page 55). When a light is shone on the reflector, the mirror and lens combine to focus and reflect the light rays back out, in the opposite direction to the way they came in. The device is called a 'cat's eye' because the eyes of a cat contain a special reflecting layer, the tapetum, so that they too 'glow' in the dark when a light is shone onto them.

Rubber pad contains two cat's eyes

Mirrored rear surface of lens

Centre of curvature of mirror and lens

Spherical lens

Incoming and reflected light path

Cast-iron base set into road surface

6 MAKING A MOTORWAY

The roadway may not look very interesting as you speed along in a car, a metre or so above it. But road surfaces are the subject of constant research and improvement. They must have a combination of good strength, resistance to wear and to extremes of temperature and frost, excellent grip for tyres in dry and wet conditions, and a certain amount of flexibility so that they do not crack and flake. The main types of road surface today are based on asphaltic concrete, which is a mix of asphalt, gravel, sand and concrete. The surface has a 'camber', that is, a slight arched or domed shape in the centre, so that water drains off the sides.

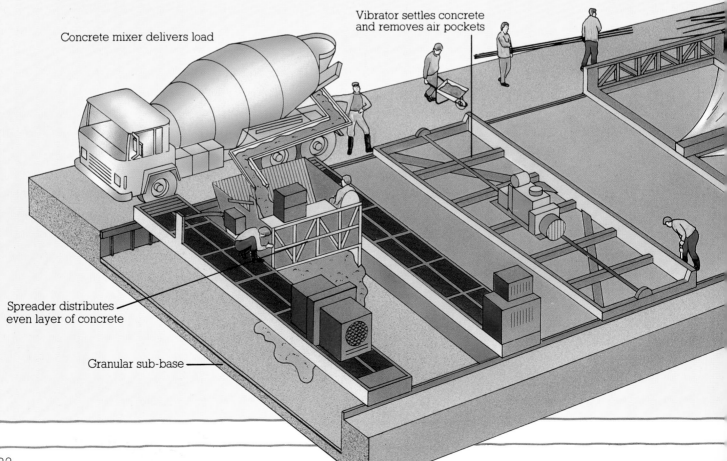

Concrete mixer delivers load

Vibrator settles concrete and removes air pockets

Spreader distributes even layer of concrete

Granular sub-base

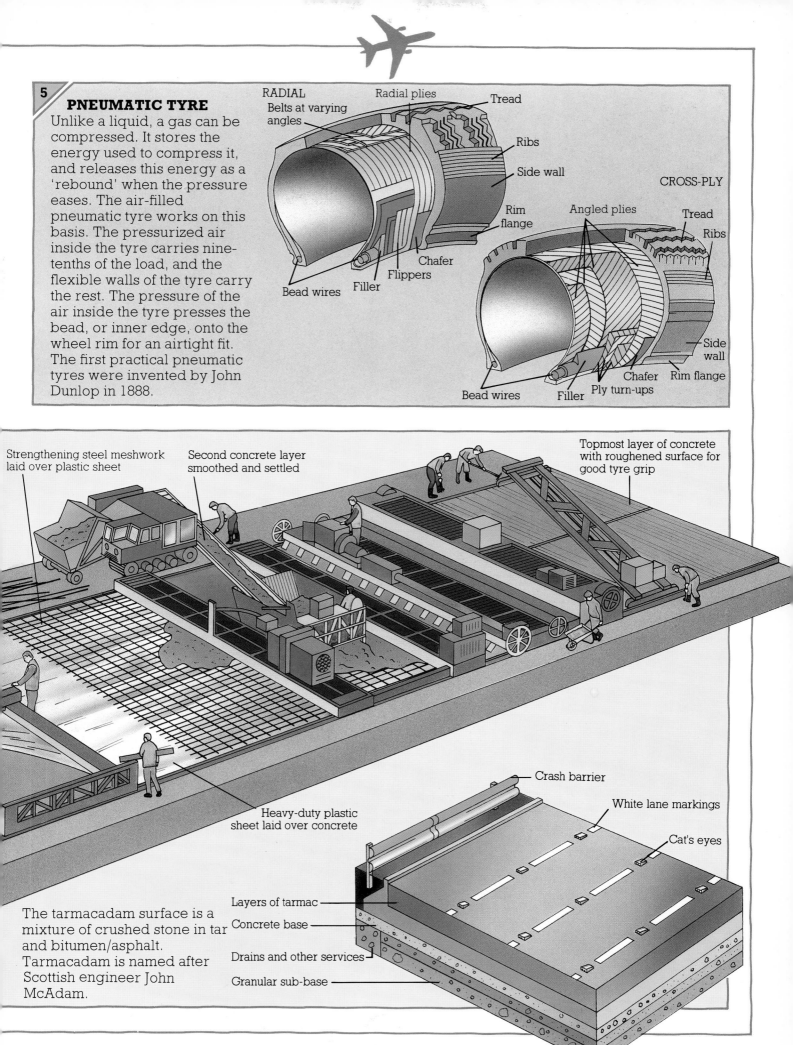

5

PNEUMATIC TYRE

Unlike a liquid, a gas can be compressed. It stores the energy used to compress it, and releases this energy as a 'rebound' when the pressure eases. The air-filled pneumatic tyre works on this basis. The pressurized air inside the tyre carries nine-tenths of the load, and the flexible walls of the tyre carry the rest. The pressure of the air inside the tyre presses the bead, or inner edge, onto the wheel rim for an airtight fit. The first practical pneumatic tyres were invented by John Dunlop in 1888.

RADIAL
Belts at varying angles
Radial plies
Tread
Ribs
Side wall
Rim flange
Chafer
Flippers
Filler
Bead wires

CROSS-PLY
Angled plies
Tread
Ribs
Side wall
Rim flange
Chafer
Ply turn-ups
Filler
Bead wires

Strengthening steel meshwork laid over plastic sheet

Second concrete layer smoothed and settled

Topmost layer of concrete with roughened surface for good tyre grip

Heavy-duty plastic sheet laid over concrete

Crash barrier

White lane markings

Cat's eyes

Layers of tarmac

Concrete base

Drains and other services

Granular sub-base

The tarmacadam surface is a mixture of crushed stone in tar and bitumen/asphalt. Tarmacadam is named after Scottish engineer John McAdam.

THE DOCKS

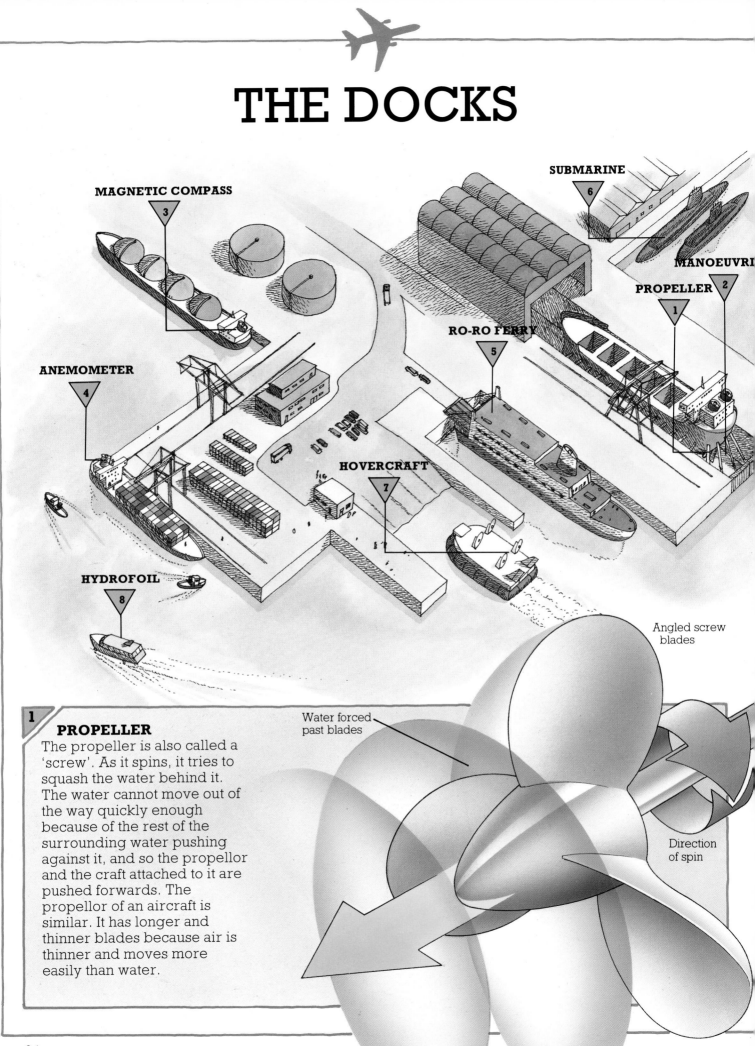

MAGNETIC COMPASS 3

SUBMARINE 6

MANOEUVRI

PROPELLER 2 1

ANEMOMETER 4

RO-RO FERRY 5

HOVERCRAFT 7

HYDROFOIL 8

Angled screw blades

Water forced past blades

Direction of spin

1 PROPELLER

The propeller is also called a 'screw'. As it spins, it tries to squash the water behind it. The water cannot move out of the way quickly enough because of the rest of the surrounding water pushing against it, and so the propellor and the craft attached to it are pushed forwards. The propellor of an aircraft is similar. It has longer and thinner blades because air is thinner and moves more easily than water.

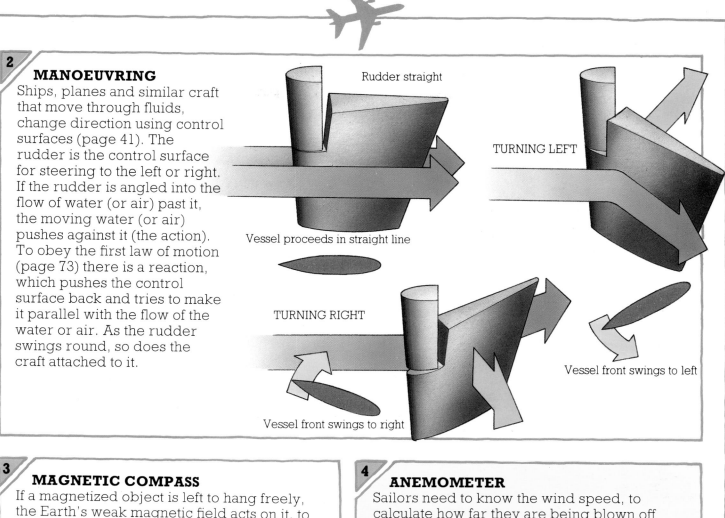

2 MANOEUVRING

Ships, planes and similar craft that move through fluids, change direction using control surfaces (page 41). The rudder is the control surface for steering to the left or right. If the rudder is angled into the flow of water (or air) past it, the moving water (or air) pushes against it (the action). To obey the first law of motion (page 73) there is a reaction, which pushes the control surface back and tries to make it parallel with the flow of the water or air. As the rudder swings round, so does the craft attached to it.

Rudder straight

Vessel proceeds in straight line

TURNING LEFT

Vessel front swings to left

TURNING RIGHT

Vessel front swings to right

3 MAGNETIC COMPASS

If a magnetized object is left to hang freely, the Earth's weak magnetic field acts on it, to make the object line up with the Earth's own lines of force. As only unlike poles of a magnet attract each other, it is the south pole of a magnetic compass that is pulled towards the Earth's own North Pole. A ship's compass floats on oil in order to remain steady in high seas.

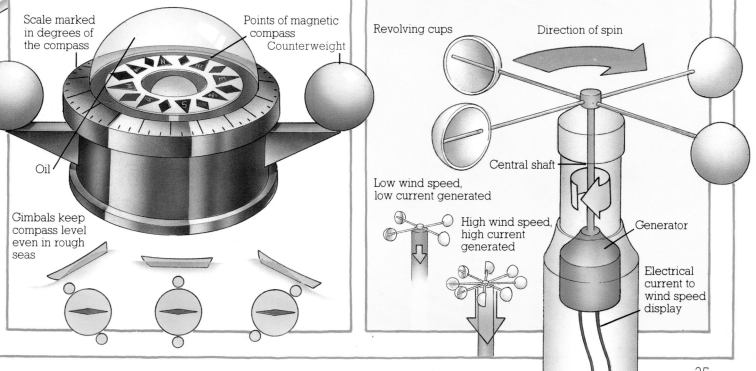

Scale marked in degrees of the compass

Points of magnetic compass

Counterweight

Oil

Gimbals keep compass level even in rough seas

4 ANEMOMETER

Sailors need to know the wind speed, to calculate how far they are being blown off course, to warn of approaching storms, or to help them decide which sails to set. The anemometer's cups are spun by the wind. The faster they spin, the more electricity is produced in the small generator, and the higher is the dial or display reading.

Revolving cups

Direction of spin

Central shaft

Low wind speed, low current generated

High wind speed, high current generated

Generator

Electrical current to wind speed display

5 RO-RO FERRY

The word ro-ro or 'Roll-On-Roll-Off' refers to the way that vehicles can drive in one end of the ferry along a ramp, and drive off a ramp at the other end, without being lifted by a crane or having to turn around inside. The ferry has propellers at both bow and stern (front and back), and often along the sides too, so that it can manoeuvre forwards, backwards and sideways. The heaviest vehicles are usually put on the ferry's lower decks. This gives the ferry a lower centre of gravity, which means that it has greater stability and is tossed around less in rough weather.

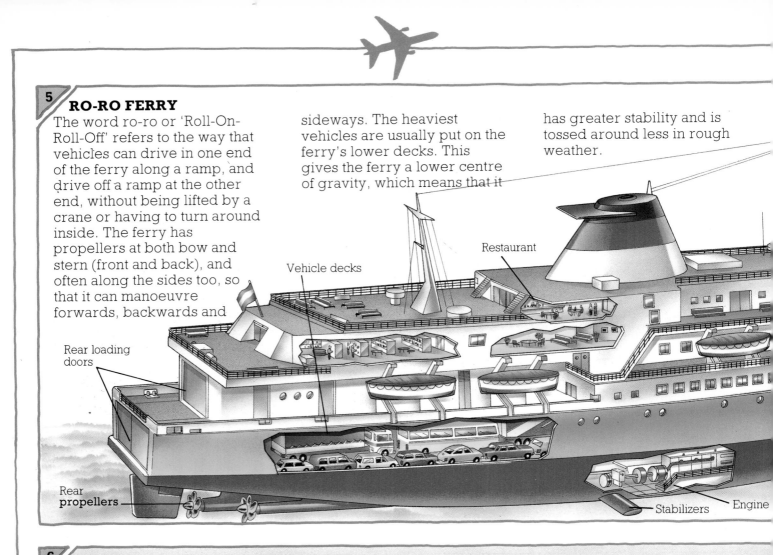

Restaurant

Vehicle decks

Rear loading doors

Rear propellers

Stabilizers

Engine

6 SUBMARINE

Curved surfaces resist pressure better than flat ones (as in the aerosol can, page 11, and the bridge arch, page 46). The submarine can withstand great pressures as it dives beneath the waves. SONAR (SOund NAvigation and Ranging) enables the submarine to navigate and detect objects under water. High-pitched 'pings' of sound are given off by the transmitter, and a series of hydrophones (underwater microphones) listens for the returning echoes. From the direction of the echoes, and the time they take to return, computers on-board the submarine can calculate an object's direction, its distance or ranging, its size and shape. In passive sonar, the submarine simply listens for noises produced by other craft.

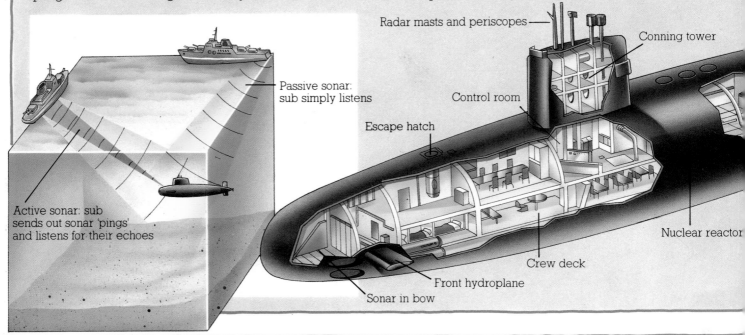

Passive sonar: sub simply listens

Active sonar: sub sends out sonar 'pings' and listens for their echoes

Radar masts and periscopes

Conning tower

Control room

Escape hatch

Nuclear reactor

Crew deck

Front hydroplane

Sonar in bow

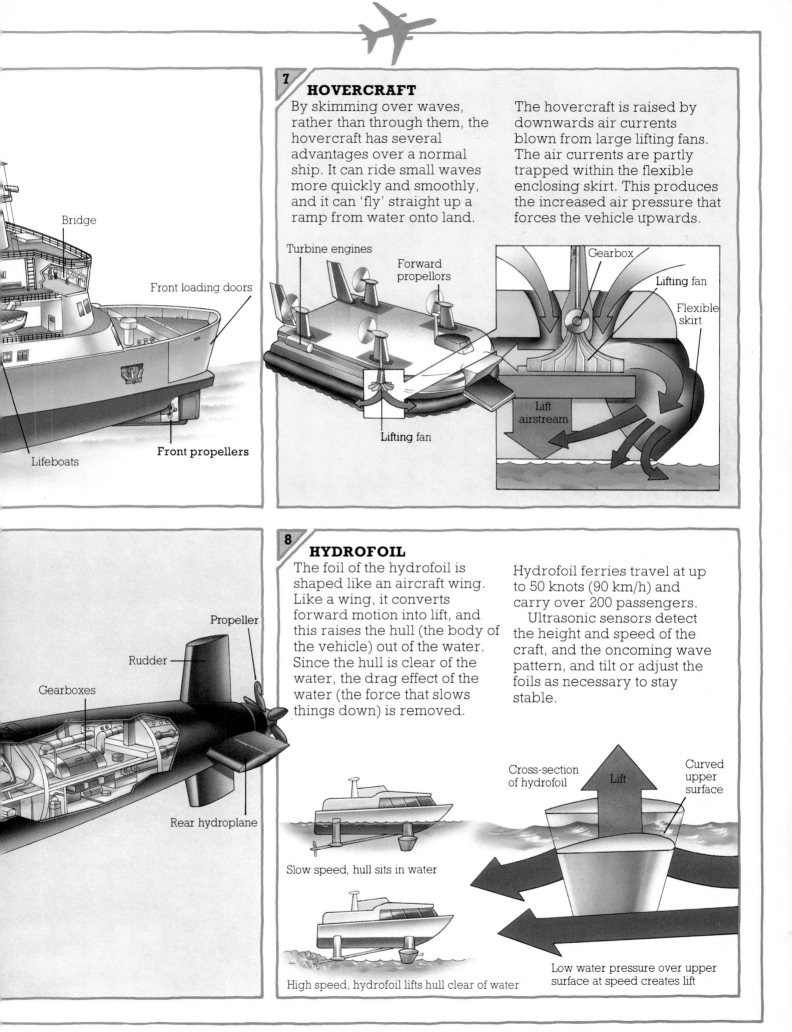

Bridge

Front loading doors

Front propellers

Lifeboats

7 HOVERCRAFT

By skimming over waves, rather than through them, the hovercraft has several advantages over a normal ship. It can ride small waves more quickly and smoothly, and it can 'fly' straight up a ramp from water onto land.

The hovercraft is raised by downwards air currents blown from large lifting fans. The air currents are partly trapped within the flexible enclosing skirt. This produces the increased air pressure that forces the vehicle upwards.

Turbine engines

Forward propellors

Lifting fan

Gearbox

Lifting fan

Flexible skirt

Lift airstream

8 HYDROFOIL

The foil of the hydrofoil is shaped like an aircraft wing. Like a wing, it converts forward motion into lift, and this raises the hull (the body of the vehicle) out of the water. Since the hull is clear of the water, the drag effect of the water (the force that slows things down) is removed.

Hydrofoil ferries travel at up to 50 knots (90 km/h) and carry over 200 passengers.

Ultrasonic sensors detect the height and speed of the craft, and the oncoming wave pattern, and tilt or adjust the foils as necessary to stay stable.

Propeller

Rudder

Gearboxes

Rear hydroplane

Slow speed, hull sits in water

High speed, hydrofoil lifts hull clear of water

Cross-section of hydrofoil

Lift

Curved upper surface

Low water pressure over upper surface at speed creates lift

ON AN AIRLINER

JUMBO JET **4**   FLIGHT-DECK **2**   RADIO AND RADAR **1**   LIFEJACKET **3**

1 RADIO AND RADAR

Aircraft navigate using radio in two ways. In RADAR (RAdio Detection And Ranging), the aircraft's transmitter sends out bursts of radio signals. These bounce off the ground and objects such as buildings and other aircraft. The aircraft detects the returning echoes with its receiver (the principle is the same as for SONAR, page 36). Radar equipment is usually hoisted in the radome, in the aircraft's nose (page 40). In addition ground stations send out radio signals. (Each station has a different code.) The receiver picks up these signals, and from their direction and strength, the flight-deck computers can pinpoint the plane's position.

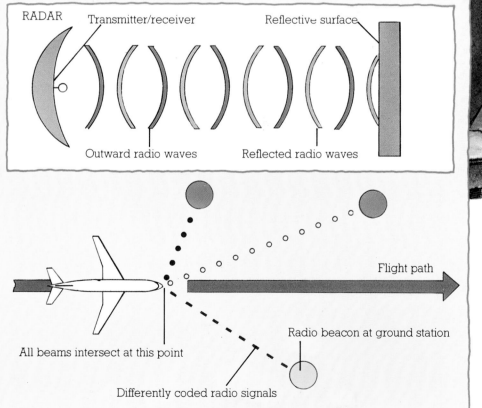

RADAR   Transmitter/receiver   Reflective surface

Outward radio waves   Reflected radio waves

Flight path

All beams intersect at this point

Radio beacon at ground station

Differently coded radio signals

2 FLIGHT-DECK

The flight-deck of a modern jetliner has dozens of displays and controls. These are carefully designed and positioned so that the crew can concentrate on the most important ones; they notice the others only if a problem arises. The airspeed indicator shows the aircraft's speed through the air. The altimeter, which uses the same principle as a *barometer*, measures height above sea level. A *gyroscope* is linked to the 'attitude display' that shows whether the aircraft is flying level or tilted to one side.

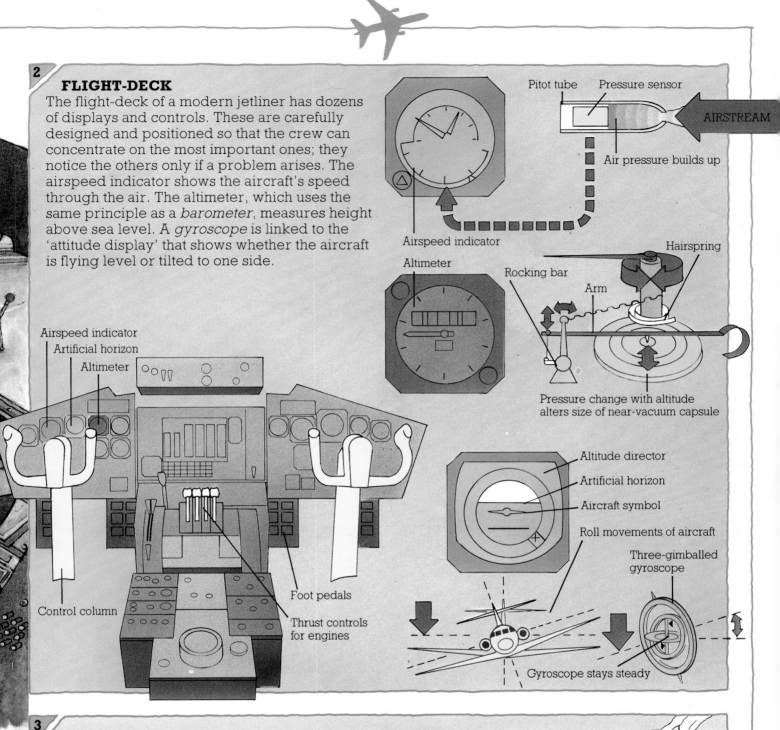

Pitot tube
Pressure sensor
AIRSTREAM
Air pressure builds up

Airspeed indicator

Altimeter

Rocking bar
Arm
Hairspring

Pressure change with altitude alters size of near-vacuum capsule

Airspeed indicator
Artificial horizon
Altimeter

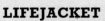

Control column

Foot pedals

Thrust controls for engines

Altitude director
Artificial horizon
Aircraft symbol
Roll movements of aircraft
Three-gimballed gyroscope

Gyroscope stays steady

3 LIFEJACKET

Airliners carry lifejackets, and instructions to show passengers how to use them, for all journeys over water. Some jackets are blown up by the wearer, while others self-inflate when a cord is pulled. When the jacket enters sea water, a chemical reaction causes a light to flash. This signals to rescuers the position of the person needing help.

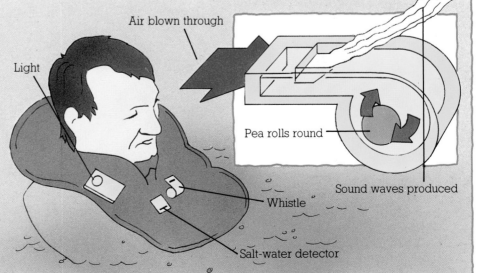

Air blown through

Light

Pea rolls round

Sound waves produced

Whistle

Salt-water detector

4 JUMBO JET

One of the most complex machines in the world, the airliner consists of several million separate parts – from turbine blades in the jet engines to passenger headphones for the movie soundtrack. The separate parts are grouped into a series of systems. The parts within each system work together to perform one overall function. The compressors, pistons and pressurized fluid in the hydraulic pipes, which work the various control surfaces and landing gear, make up the *hydraulic system*. The hundreds of kilometres of wiring that connect different parts all over the aircraft to the flight-deck controls and displays, make up the *electrical system*. The fuel tanks, pumps and pipes comprise the *fuel system*. The structural parts such as the fuselage, wings, tailplane and fin, make up the *airframe*.

Cruising at 1000 kilometres per hour, ten kilometres up, an airliner's wing provides lift. When the plane takes off or comes in to land, various parts of its wing lift away. The shape of the wing as seen from the side – called the aerofoil section – changes, according to the speed of the aircraft. Spoilers on top of the wing 'spoil', or interrupt, the airflow over the wing, while slats at the front and flaps at the back give extra lift at slower speeds.

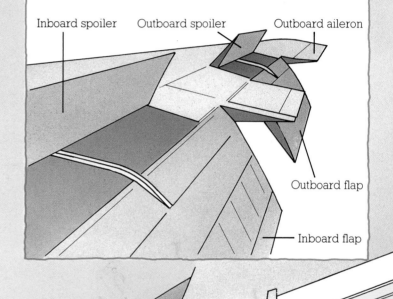

Inboard spoiler   Outboard spoiler   Outboard aileron

Outboard flap

Inboard flap

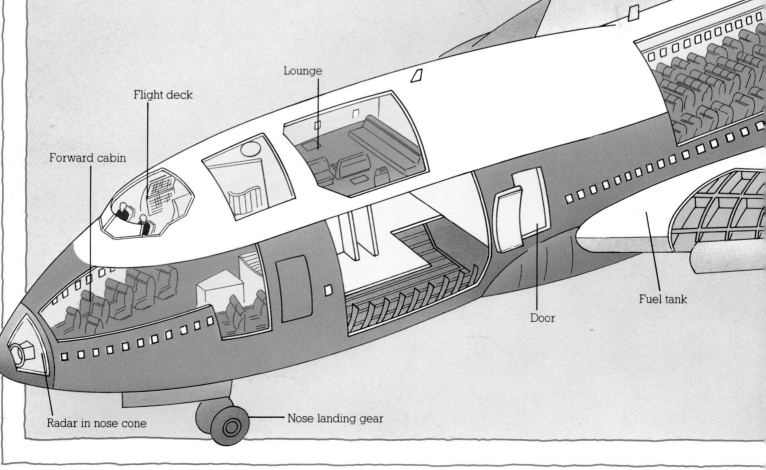

Lounge

Flight deck

Forward cabin

Door

Fuel tank

Radar in nose cone   Nose landing gear

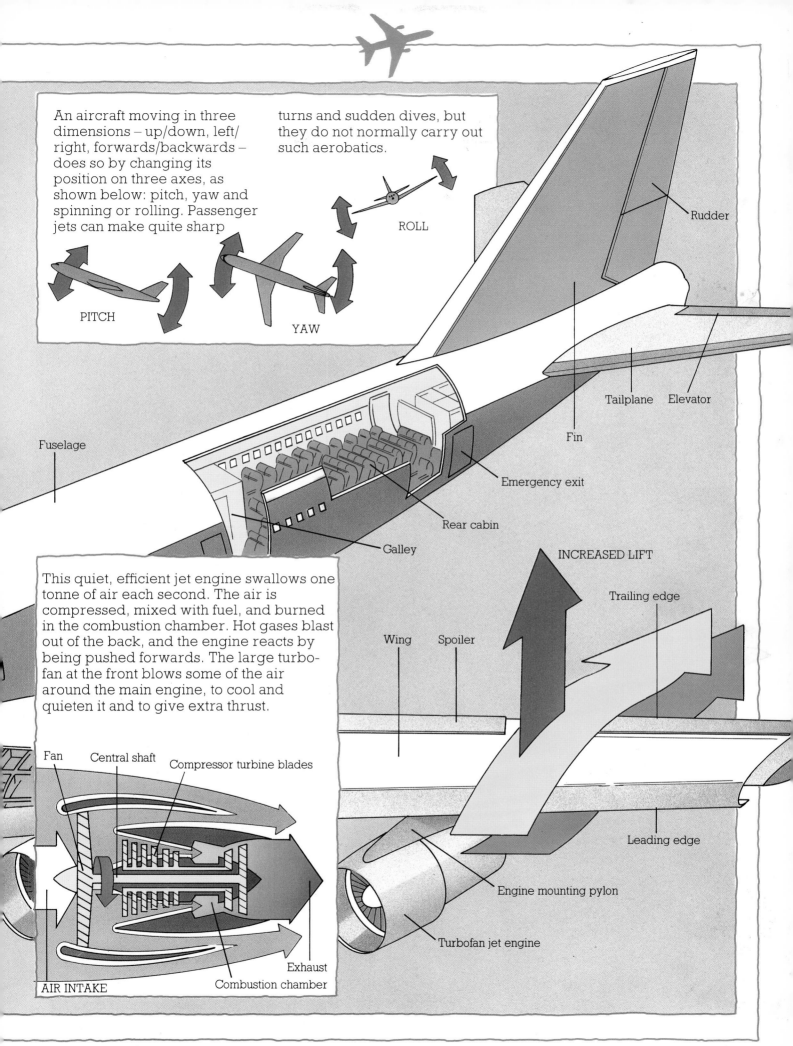

An aircraft moving in three dimensions – up/down, left/right, forwards/backwards – does so by changing its position on three axes, as shown below: pitch, yaw and spinning or rolling. Passenger jets can make quite sharp turns and sudden dives, but they do not normally carry out such aerobatics.

ROLL

PITCH

YAW

Rudder

Tailplane   Elevator

Fin

Emergency exit

Fuselage

Rear cabin

Galley

INCREASED LIFT

Trailing edge

Wing   Spoiler

This quiet, efficient jet engine swallows one tonne of air each second. The air is compressed, mixed with fuel, and burned in the combustion chamber. Hot gases blast out of the back, and the engine reacts by being pushed forwards. The large turbo-fan at the front blows some of the air around the main engine, to cool and quieten it and to give extra thrust.

Leading edge

Fan   Central shaft   Compressor turbine blades

Engine mounting pylon

Turbofan jet engine

Exhaust

AIR INTAKE   Combustion chamber

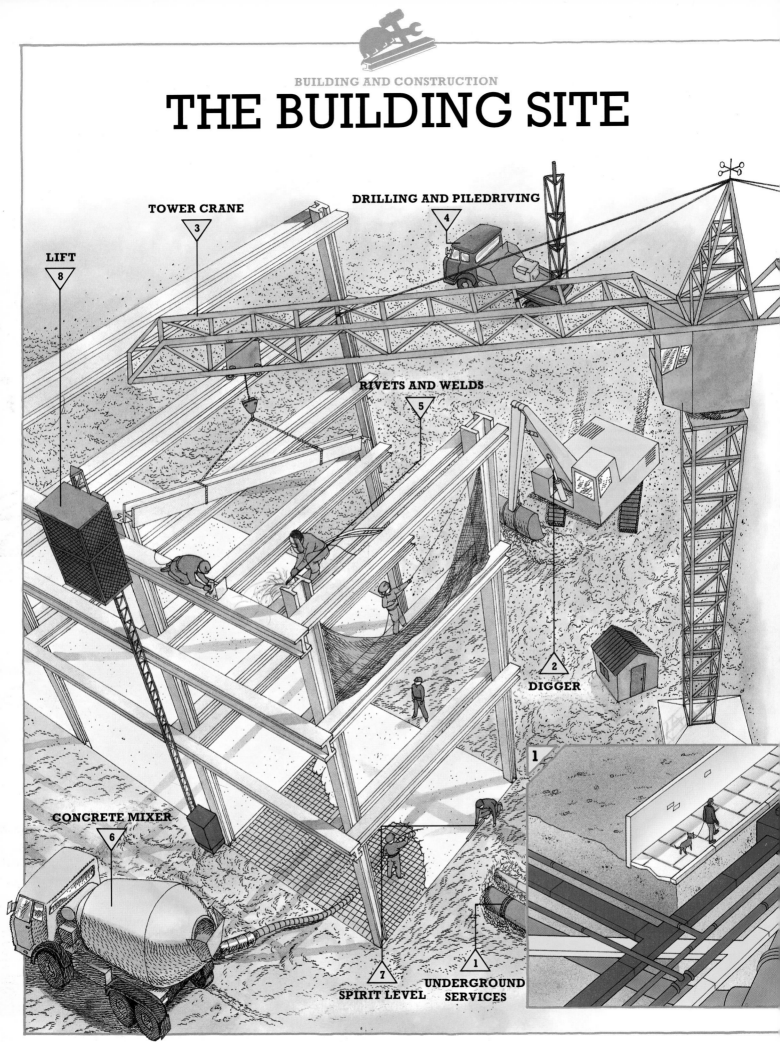

BUILDING AND CONSTRUCTION

THE BUILDING SITE

TOWER CRANE
3

DRILLING AND PILEDRIVING
4

LIFT
8

RIVETS AND WELDS
5

DIGGER
2

CONCRETE MIXER
6

SPIRIT LEVEL
7

UNDERGROUND
SERVICES
1

2 DIGGER

The multipurpose digger makes trenches and holes, loads materials into trucks, and can bulldoze areas level. The arms, and their buckets, are operated by hydraulic pistons. As hydraulic fluid is pumped under great pressure into the cylinder, it pushes the piston along. The piston is connected to a lever that moves the arm or bucket. These hydraulic pistons can only push. Like the muscles in the human body they are arranged in opposing pairs.

3 TOWER CRANE

Towering over the building site, this crane can lift objects over a large area. Its main jib swivels round, and the hook-carrying trolley is winched along the jib by cables and a motor. The crane is 'self-erecting'. After its base is installed, it uses a special extending section, into which it fits a new section of tower. The extending section then 'crawls' up the tower section, fits another tower section into itself and so on, until it is the correct height.

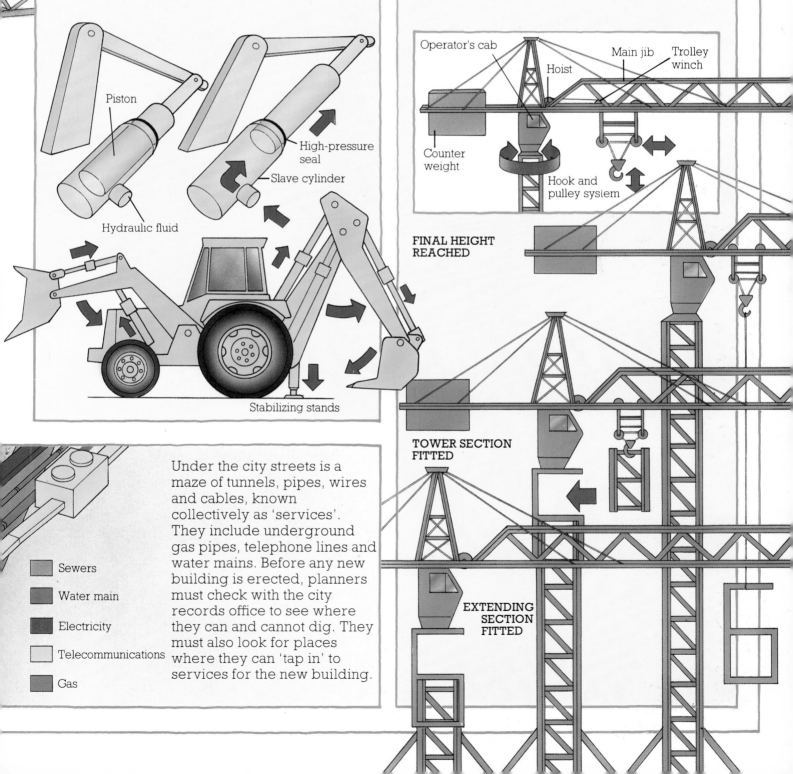

Piston

High-pressure seal

Slave cylinder

Hydraulic fluid

Stabilizing stands

Operator's cab

Hoist

Main jib

Trolley winch

Counter weight

Hook and pulley system

FINAL HEIGHT REACHED

TOWER SECTION FITTED

EXTENDING SECTION FITTED

Under the city streets is a maze of tunnels, pipes, wires and cables, known collectively as 'services'. They include underground gas pipes, telephone lines and water mains. Before any new building is erected, planners must check with the city records office to see where they can and cannot dig. They must also look for places where they can 'tap in' to services for the new building.

- Sewers
- Water main
- Electricity
- Telecommunications
- Gas

4 ▸ DRILLING AND PILEDRIVING

To stop a building toppling, cracking or sinking, it must be built on firm foundations. The taller the building, the deeper the foundations. Columns or piles can be sunk deep into the ground by drilling or driving. The piledriver is a large weight that is repeatedly raised and dropped onto a driving wedge or pile, hammering it deep into the earth. The earthdrill, a rotary device in a derrick tower, works like an oil rig drill. London's tallest building, Canary Wharf Tower, stands on 222 piles, each 2 metres across and 20 metres deep.

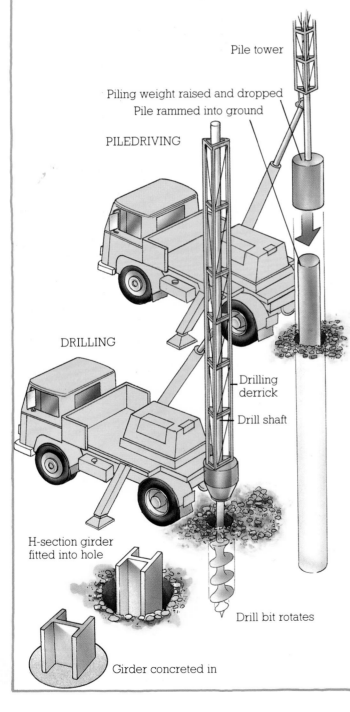

Pile tower

Piling weight raised and dropped
Pile rammed into ground

PILEDRIVING

DRILLING

Drilling derrick

Drill shaft

H-section girder fitted into hole

Drill bit rotates

Girder concreted in

5 ▸ RIVETS AND WELDS

There are numerous ways of joining girders, plates and other pieces of buildings and machinery. These include screws, nuts and bolts, adhesives, rivets and welds. A rivet is a metal pin with a flattened head at one end. It is pushed by its flat head into holes in the parts to be fastened. A rivet gun then hammers the other

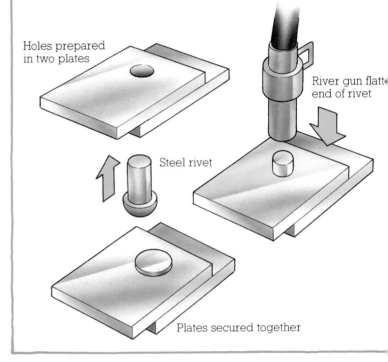

Holes prepared in two plates

River gun flatt end of rivet

Steel rivet

Plates secured together

6 ▸ CONCRETE MIXER

In a premixed concrete truck, the Archimedes screw keeps the concrete or mortar circulating as it is carried from the mixing depot to the building site. The screw is essentially a spiral or helical ramp (page 12) wound around inside a drum. The same device was used in Ancient Egypt, to lift water out of ditches for irrigating the fields beyond.

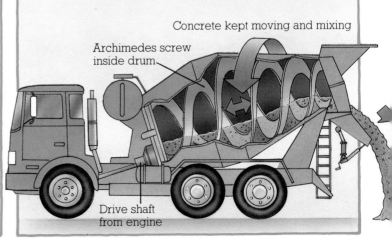

Concrete kept moving and mixing

Archimedes screw inside drum

Drive shaft from engine

end flat, squeezing and securing the parts together.

In welding, the very high temperature created by an electric arc or flame melts the two metal parts where they touch. The liquefied metals run together, and after the heat is removed they solidify and fuse together.

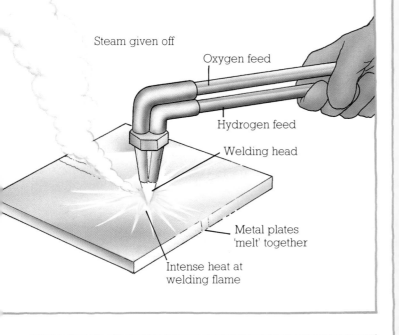

Steam given off

Oxygen feed

Hydrogen feed

Welding head

Metal plates 'melt' together

Intense heat at welding flame

SPIRIT LEVEL

7

In the spirit level, a bubble of air floats in oil or a spirit-based fluid, inside a transparent container. The air, being much less dense than the fluid, always finds the highest part of the container and floats on top of the fluid. When the device is level, the bubble rests in the middle of the container.

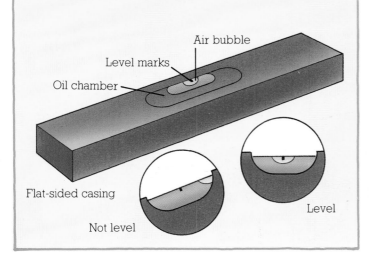

Air bubble

Level marks

Oil chamber

Flat-sided casing

Not level

Level

LIFT

8

The goods and materials lift on a building site works in the same way as the passenger lift inside a tall building. The lift car runs up and down a guide tower, or between the guide rails of a lift shaft. It is winched up by the lifting motor, which does not have to lift the whole weight of the car since this is balanced by a counterweight. A safety brake locks the car to the rails or tower if the cable snaps.

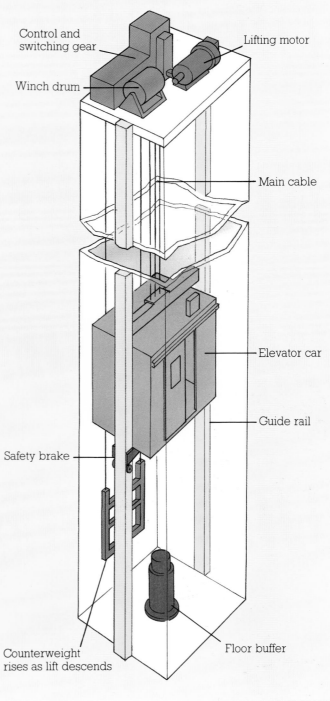

Control and switching gear

Lifting motor

Winch drum

Main cable

Elevator car

Guide rail

Safety brake

Counterweight rises as lift descends

Floor buffer

BRIDGES

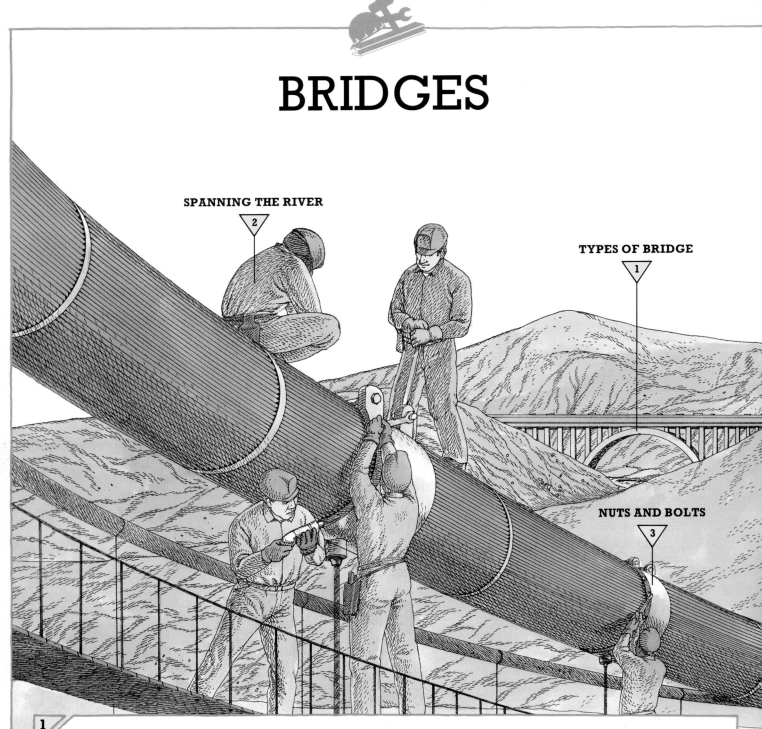

SPANNING THE RIVER
2

TYPES OF BRIDGE
1

NUTS AND BOLTS
3

1 **TYPES OF BRIDGE**

Four main types of bridge design are shown on the right. Each has advantages. The beam design can be simple and inexpensive, but it needs regular supports along its length. It is not suitable for a wide, deep river. In the cantilever design, each pair of side spans projects beyond their supporting tower, balancing each other for better stability.

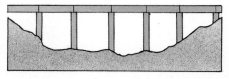
Beam

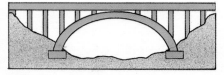
Single-span arch

Suspension

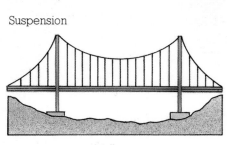

Cantilever

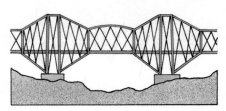

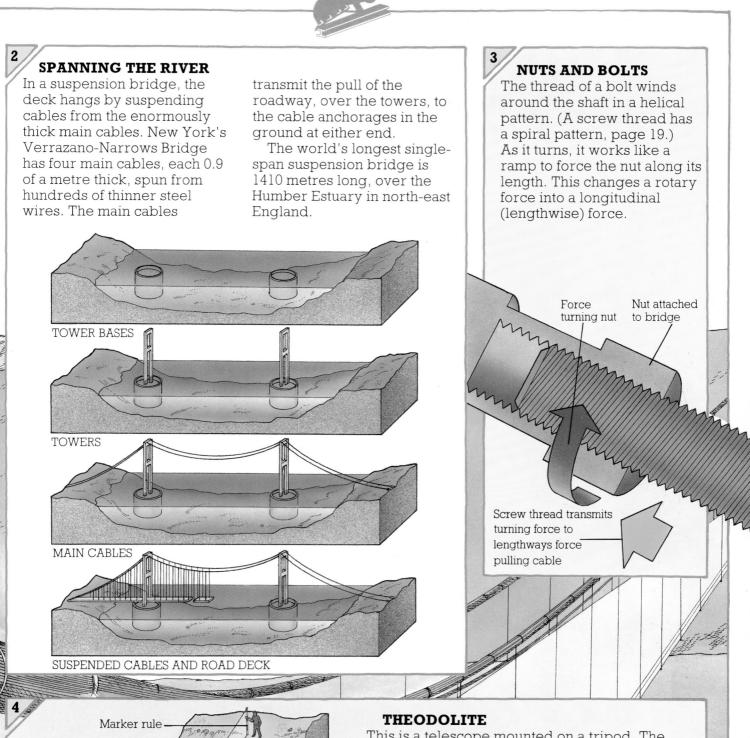

2 SPANNING THE RIVER

In a suspension bridge, the deck hangs by suspending cables from the enormously thick main cables. New York's Verrazano-Narrows Bridge has four main cables, each 0.9 of a metre thick, spun from hundreds of thinner steel wires. The main cables transmit the pull of the roadway, over the towers, to the cable anchorages in the ground at either end.

The world's longest single-span suspension bridge is 1410 metres long, over the Humber Estuary in north-east England.

TOWER BASES

TOWERS

MAIN CABLES

SUSPENDED CABLES AND ROAD DECK

3 NUTS AND BOLTS

The thread of a bolt winds around the shaft in a helical pattern. (A screw thread has a spiral pattern, page 19.) As it turns, it works like a ramp to force the nut along its length. This changes a rotary force into a longitudinal (lengthwise) force.

Force turning nut

Nut attached to bridge

Screw thread transmits turning force to lengthways force pulling cable

4 THEODOLITE

Marker rule

Angle measured between marks on rule

Theodolite

This is a telescope mounted on a tripod. The first target is sighted through the eyepiece. Then the telescope is swung up or down, or to one side, to sight a second target. The angle between these two targets is read off scales. They surveyor then uses geometry to calculate distance. Laser theodolites use a laser to measure distances and angles more accurately than the optical theodolite.

TUNNELS

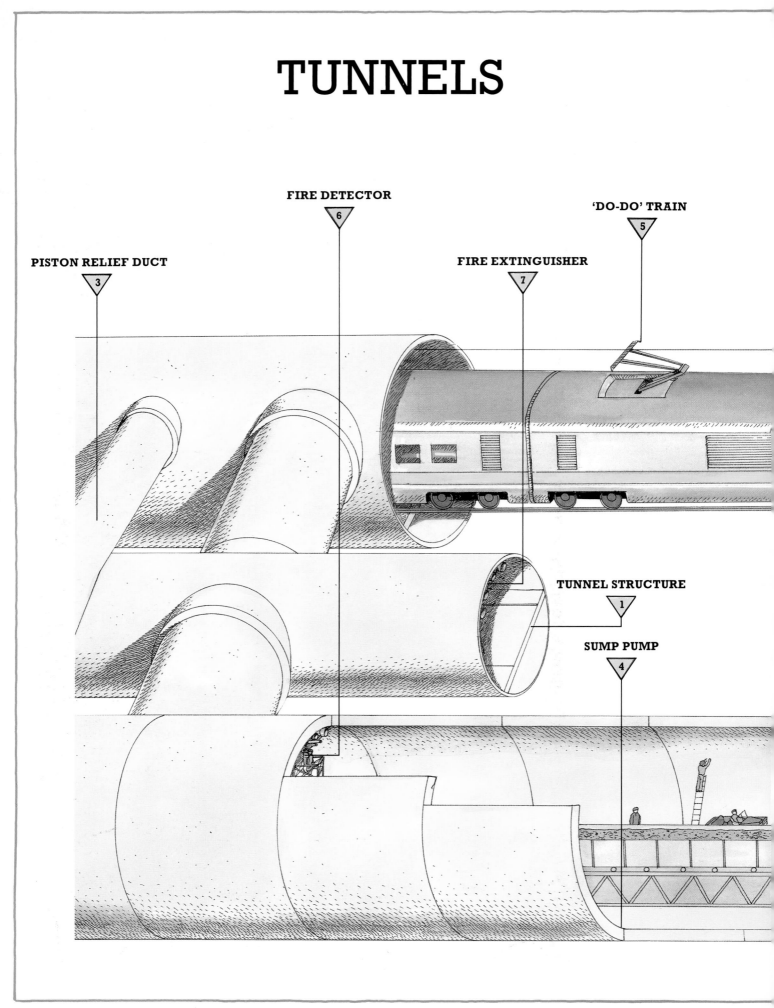

PISTON RELIEF DUCT 3

FIRE DETECTOR 6

'DO-DO' TRAIN 5

FIRE EXTINGUISHER 7

TUNNEL STRUCTURE 1

SUMP PUMP 4

1 TUNNEL STRUCTURE

The Eurotunnel between Britain and France is, in fact, three tunnels. The two main shafts, each 7.6 metres across, convey electric locomotives pulling wagons of vehicles, freight and passengers. Between them is the smaller service tunnel, 4.8 metres in diameter. This houses services such as electrical cables and water pipes. It can also be used for access and maintenance, and escape in emergencies.

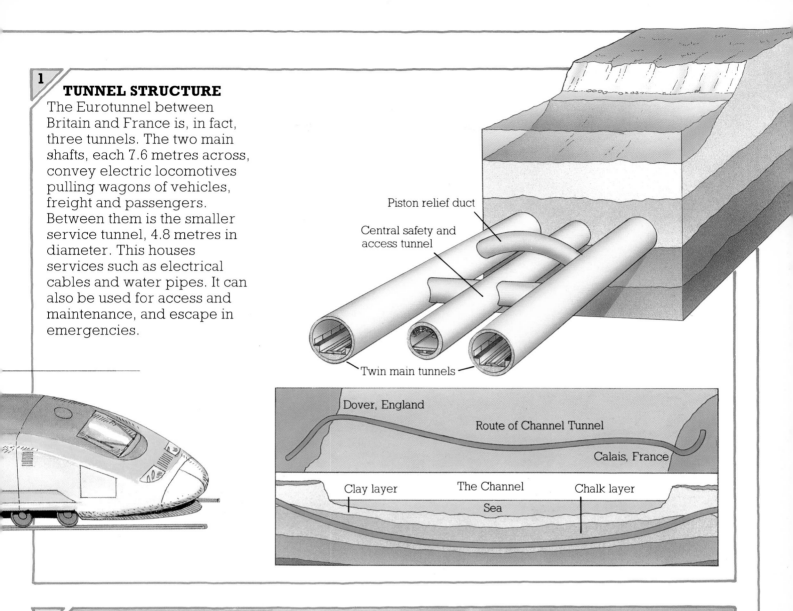

Piston relief duct

Central safety and access tunnel

Twin main tunnels

Dover, England

Route of Channel Tunnel

Calais, France

Clay layer   The Channel   Chalk layer

Sea

2

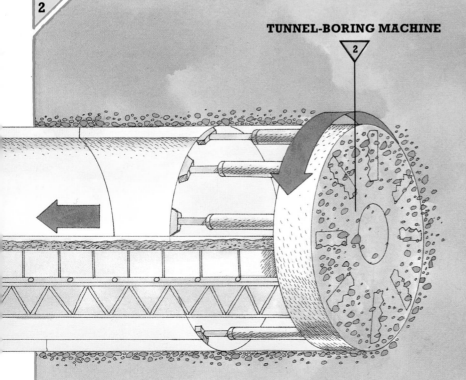

TUNNEL-BORING MACHINE

TUNNEL-BORING MACHINE

Eurotunnel's rotating cutter head was like a giant drill (page 21). With over 100 cutting rollers to chew up the rock, and 200 teeth, made of the very hard metal tungsten. The head rotated about twice each minute, depending on the material being drilled. Hydraulic rams guided the cutting head, steered by laser beams. The gripper ring pushed against the tunnel wall as rams forced the machine forwards. A system of conveyors took away the spoil at a rate of 70 cubic metres (almost two large dumper trucks) for every one metre of tunnel drilled.

3 PISTON RELIEF DUCT

As a train travels through the Eurotunnel at 160 kilometres per hour, it pushes air in front of it. This gradually increases the air pressure, like air being forced along a cylinder by a piston (page 67). It could even damage passengers' ears. So there are regular smaller cross-shafts, known as *piston relief ducts*, between the two main tunnels. Air pushed by the speeding locomotive circulates through these, back along the other tunnel, and then into the main tunnel behind the locomotive. In this way the pressure build-up is avoided.

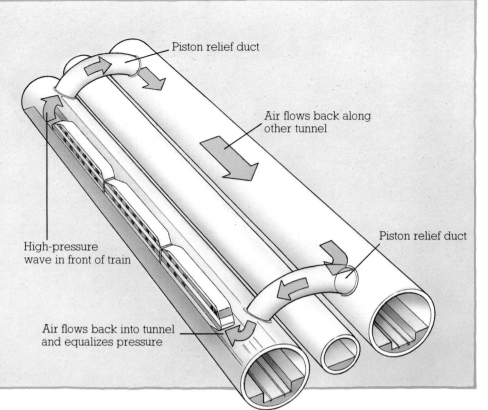

Piston relief duct

Air flows back along other tunnel

Piston relief duct

High-pressure wave in front of train

Air flows back into tunnel and equalizes pressure

4 SUMP PUMP

It is impossible to prevent rainwater, drips of oil and fuel, and various other fluids from collecting along the tunnel bottoms. Among other problems, this could create a fire hazard. The sump pump is specially designed to collect these various wastes. It is worked by high-pressure water that rotates the vanes and draws up the wastes, to be pumped away along the outlet pipe.

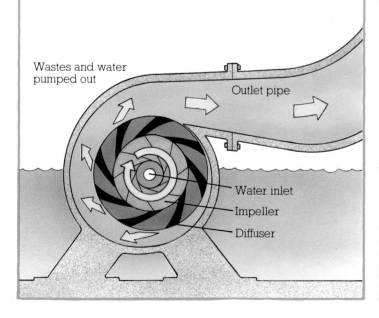

Wastes and water pumped out

Outlet pipe

Water inlet

Impeller

Diffuser

5 'DO-DO' TRAIN

The rail trip under the Channel itself takes only 35 minutes. Like the Ro-Ro ferry (page 36), the Do-Do train is designed for a speedy and convenient turnaround of vehicles and freight. Cars can 'Drive On and Drive Off' without having to be loaded by cranes or turn around in

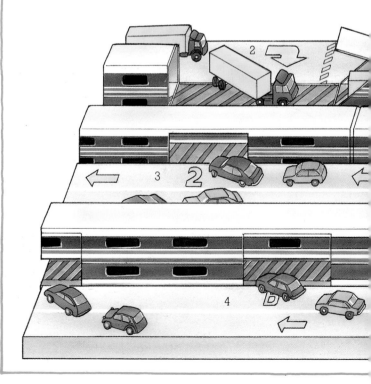

6 FIRE DETECTOR

The fire detectors are fitted at regular intervals along the tunnel. They contain a specially-developed *alloy* (mixture of metals) that melts at temperatures only a little above normal. The melted blob completes an electric circuit and sets off the alarm.

Power source

Alarm

Circuit wiring

Electric wire

Alloy in thimble

Melted alloy completes circuit to set off alarm

Heat sensor

HEAT

7 FIRE EXTINGUISHER

This is a carbon dioxide (CO_2)-type extinguisher. When the strike knob is hit, the piercer punctures the pressure-release disc and allows the pressurized carbon dioxide to escape. This gas is heavier than air and it settles over the fire, smothering it like a blanket, and keeping away the oxygen that flames need to burn. Deprived of oxygen, the fire gradually goes out.

Carbon dioxide 'blanket' smothers fire

Directing tube

Strike knob

Piercer

Pressure release disc

Carbon dioxide

Pressurized powder and carbon dioxide

Central tube

wagons. There are about 30 wagons in the standard tourist 'shuttle train', which travels back and forth between the two terminals. There are also the Eurostar trains for carrying passengers without vehicles.

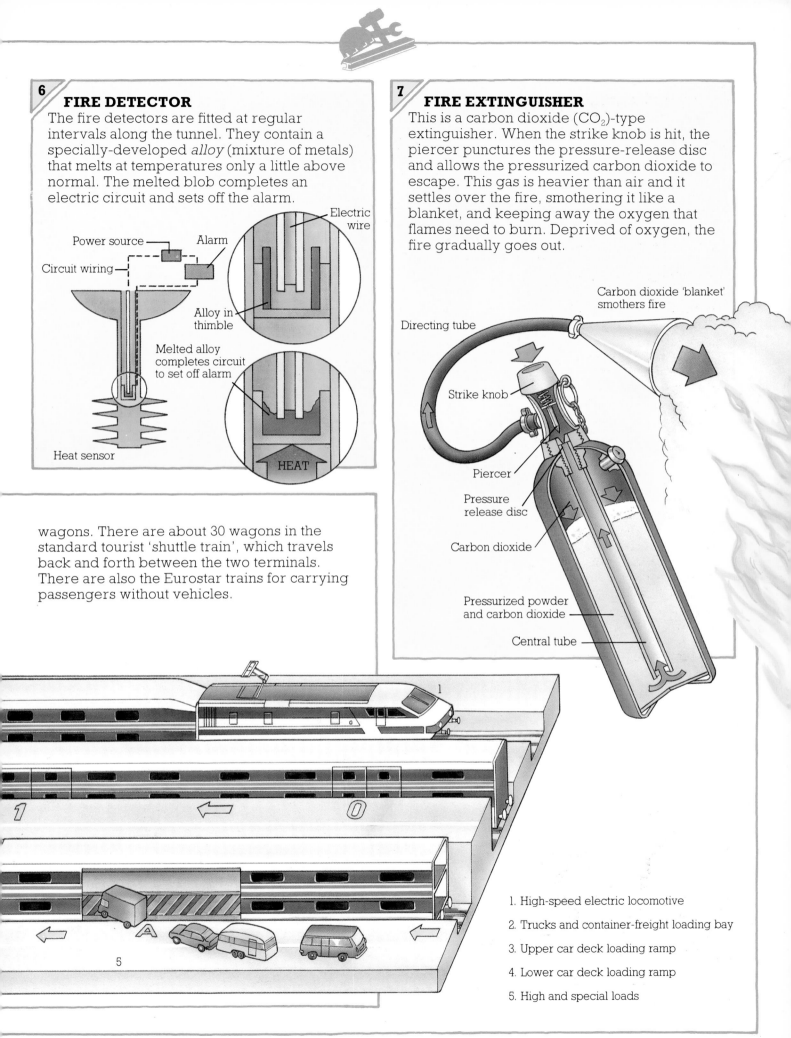

1. High-speed electric locomotive

2. Trucks and container-freight loading bay

3. Upper car deck loading ramp

4. Lower car deck loading ramp

5. High and special loads

THE NEWSROOM

BINOCULARS
7

OPTICAL FIBRE
2

COMPUTER PRINTERS
6

TELEPHONE
1

BALLPOINT PEN
4

FAX MAC

SLR CAMERA
8

MOBILE PHONE
3

1

TELEPHONE

The microphone and loudspeakers in a hi-fi system (page 79) deal with a wide range of notes, from bass drum to piccolo. But the telephone handles a relatively small range of notes, centred around the pitch of the human voice. Its working parts are therefore small and of simple construction. In the mouthpiece, sound waves vibrate the diaphragm, which compresses a packet of carbon granules. This alters the flow of electricity through the granules, producing signals that travel to the listener's earpiece.

Signals travel both ways to each phone

Telephone exchange

MOUTHPIECE

EARPIECE
Diaphragm
Armature
Wiring Coils

Electromagnet
Diaphragm
Carbon granules
Electrical current

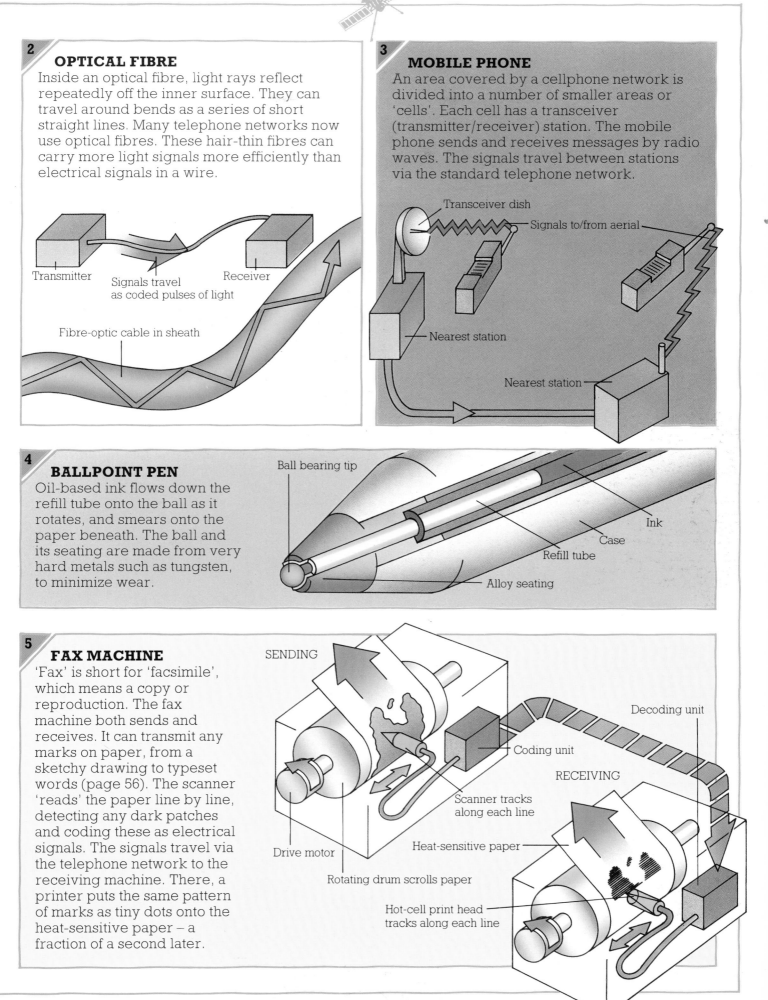

2 OPTICAL FIBRE

Inside an optical fibre, light rays reflect repeatedly off the inner surface. They can travel around bends as a series of short straight lines. Many telephone networks now use optical fibres. These hair-thin fibres can carry more light signals more efficiently than electrical signals in a wire.

Transmitter

Signals travel as coded pulses of light

Receiver

Fibre-optic cable in sheath

3 MOBILE PHONE

An area covered by a cellphone network is divided into a number of smaller areas or 'cells'. Each cell has a transceiver (transmitter/receiver) station. The mobile phone sends and receives messages by radio waves. The signals travel between stations via the standard telephone network.

Transceiver dish

Signals to/from aerial

Nearest station

Nearest station

4 BALLPOINT PEN

Oil-based ink flows down the refill tube onto the ball as it rotates, and smears onto the paper beneath. The ball and its seating are made from very hard metals such as tungsten, to minimize wear.

Ball bearing tip

Ink

Case

Refill tube

Alloy seating

5 FAX MACHINE

'Fax' is short for 'facsimile', which means a copy or reproduction. The fax machine both sends and receives. It can transmit any marks on paper, from a sketchy drawing to typeset words (page 56). The scanner 'reads' the paper line by line, detecting any dark patches and coding these as electrical signals. The signals travel via the telephone network to the receiving machine. There, a printer puts the same pattern of marks as tiny dots onto the heat-sensitive paper – a fraction of a second later.

SENDING

Decoding unit

Coding unit

RECEIVING

Scanner tracks along each line

Heat-sensitive paper

Drive motor

Rotating drum scrolls paper

Hot-cell print head tracks along each line

6 COMPUTER PRINTERS

In the printout from a dot-matrix printer, the words are made up from patterns of tiny dots. Little pins in the print head hammer against an inked ribbon as the head whizzes along, making ink spots on the paper. The pins are worked by tiny electromagnets. In a daisy-wheel printer, each letter is a raised ridge on the print head.

In a bubble-jet printer, patterns of tiny dots are made by spraying ink at the paper from a row of tiny tubes. A laser printer forms words and pictures by scanning a charged drum with a laser to change the pattern of charges on it. Dry toner powder sticks to some parts of the drum and this is transferred to a sheet of paper.

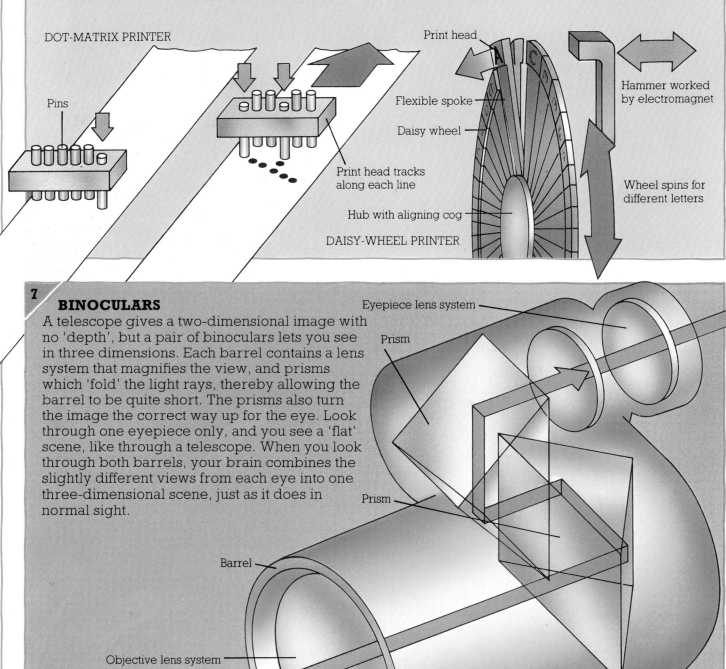

DOT-MATRIX PRINTER

Pins

Print head tracks along each line

Print head

Flexible spoke

Daisy wheel

Hub with aligning cog

DAISY-WHEEL PRINTER

Hammer worked by electromagnet

Wheel spins for different letters

7 BINOCULARS

A telescope gives a two-dimensional image with no 'depth', but a pair of binoculars lets you see in three dimensions. Each barrel contains a lens system that magnifies the view, and prisms which 'fold' the light rays, thereby allowing the barrel to be quite short. The prisms also turn the image the correct way up for the eye. Look through one eyepiece only, and you see a 'flat' scene, like through a telescope. When you look through both barrels, your brain combines the slightly different views from each eye into one three-dimensional scene, just as it does in normal sight.

Eyepiece lens system

Prism

Prism

Barrel

Objective lens system

LIGHT

SLR CAMERA

SLR means Single Lens Reflex. The 'single lens' refers to the fact that the scene through the viewfinder is exactly the same as the scene that appears on the film, because they are both seen through the same lens. (In some cameras, the viewfinder has a separate lens, to one side of the main lens.) This is achieved by a mirror in front of the film, that reflects light rays up to a five-sided pentaprism. The prism turns the image the correct way up by reflecting the light rays around a series of corners – this is the 'reflex' part. It then sends the rays on to the eye. When the shutter button is pressed, the mirror swings up out of the way, and the light rays momentarily fall onto the film before the mirror swings down again.

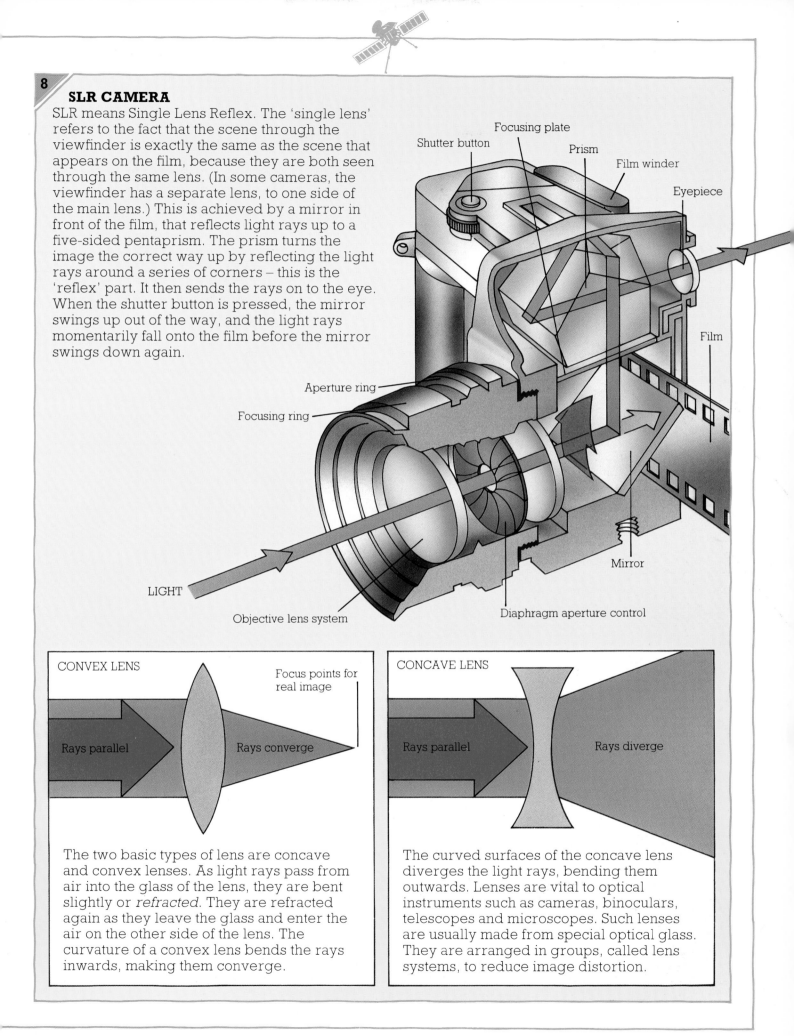

Focusing plate

Shutter button

Prism

Film winder

Eyepiece

Film

Aperture ring

Focusing ring

LIGHT

Objective lens system

Diaphragm aperture control

Mirror

CONVEX LENS

Focus points for real image

Rays parallel

Rays converge

The two basic types of lens are concave and convex lenses. As light rays pass from air into the glass of the lens, they are bent slightly or *refracted*. They are refracted again as they leave the glass and enter the air on the other side of the lens. The curvature of a convex lens bends the rays inwards, making them converge.

CONCAVE LENS

Rays parallel

Rays diverge

The curved surfaces of the concave lens diverges the light rays, bending them outwards. Lenses are vital to optical instruments such as cameras, binoculars, telescopes and microscopes. Such lenses are usually made from special optical glass. They are arranged in groups, called lens systems, to reduce image distortion.

PRINTING A BOOK

TYPESETTER **1**

COLOUR SCANNER **2**

PRINTING METHODS **3**

COLOUR PRINTING **4**

PRINTING PRESS **5**

PHOTOCOPIER **6**

1 TYPESETTER

Printed words like the ones you are reading now are the result of a series of processes, starting with the typesetter. This machine stores in its computer memory the sizes and shapes of various typefaces – the different styles and 'designs' of letters and numbers. The words in this book are in the typeface called Rockwell.

To typeset the letters, the computer controls the movements of a laser beam that transfers the shapes of the letters onto a rotating drum of special printing paper or printing film (page 58). Highly magnified, the letters are seen to be made up of numerous lines (*below*).

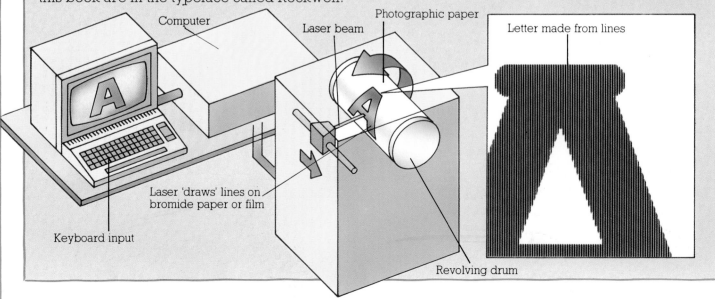

Computer

Laser beam

Photographic paper

Letter made from lines

Laser 'draws' lines on bromide paper or film

Keyboard input

Revolving drum

2 COLOUR SCANNER

To prepare a colour photograph or illustration for printing, it must first be 'separated' into its primary colours, so that each may be printed separately (page 58). This is a job for the colour scanner. The laser beam scans line by line as the photograph revolves on a drum. During the scan the different frequencies of the light in the laser correspond with each of the primary colours, so that they detect only the parts of the photograph which are of that particular colour. The different frequencies pick up each of the three primary colours – cyan (blue), magenta (red), and yellow – plus all of these for black. The information about which colours are where on the photograph is coded as electrical signals. It can be converted into four separate printing films, or stored in a computer memory, or sent to another computer or printer.

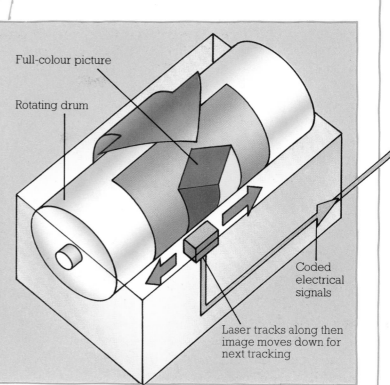

Full-colour picture

Rotating drum

Coded electrical signals

Laser tracks along then image moves down for next tracking

3 PRINTING METHODS

Since the German goldsmith Johann Gutenberg invented the first proper printing press, in about 1450, there have been various developments in printing techniques. Four methods of printing are shown here. Each depends on passing paper over an inked roller or plate, so that the ink comes off the roller or plate and sticks to the paper. Offset lithography is described on page 58. In letterpress, the image exists as a raised area on a lower base. Only the raised part receives the printing ink. In gravure, the image is a shallow 'hole' below the surface of the plate or roller, and ink is scraped from the raised, non-printing part by a doctor blade. Silk-screen printing involves forcing ink through a very fine net-like screen onto the paper; the shape of the stencil forms the image.

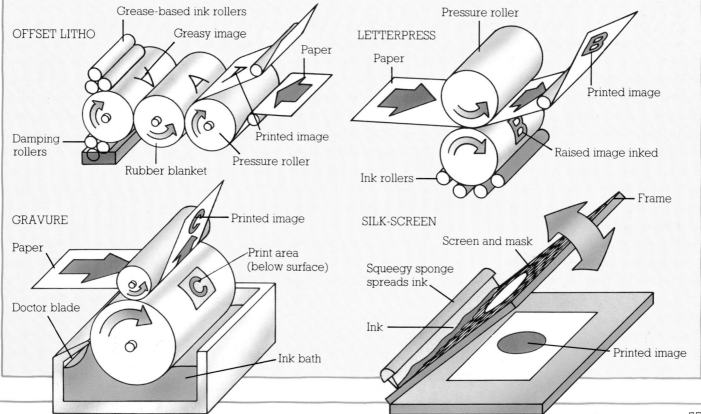

OFFSET LITHO

Grease-based ink rollers

Greasy image

Paper

Damping rollers

Rubber blanket

Printed image

Pressure roller

LETTERPRESS

Pressure roller

Paper

Printed image

Raised image inked

Ink rollers

GRAVURE

Paper

Printed image

Print area (below surface)

Doctor blade

Ink bath

SILK-SCREEN

Frame

Screen and mask

Squeegy sponge spreads ink

Ink

Printed image

4 COLOUR PRINTING

The colour pictures in this book are made from patterns of tiny ink dots. There are four colours of dots. These are the three primary printing colours of cyan, magenta and yellow, plus black. Each is printed from a separate piece of printing film on the press (*shown below*). From a distance, the eye sees the separate dots as areas of continuous ink. It also merges the different combinations of primary colours to see all the other colours of the spectrum.

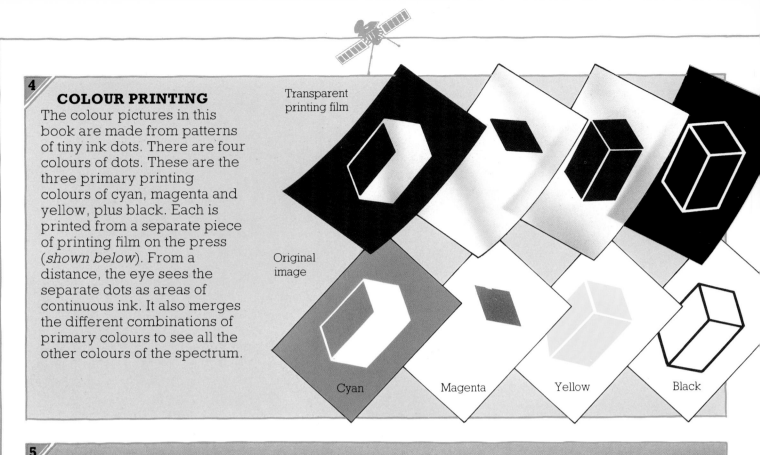

Transparent printing film

Original image

Cyan   Magenta   Yellow   Black

5 PRINTING PRESS

On the offset lithography press, each primary colour is printed separately. The image on the plate or roller exists as a part of its surface that has been treated, or 'etched', to attract grease-based printing ink – and to repel water. For areas that are not to be printed, the surface is treated to attract water but to repel the greasy ink. Damping rollers wet the non-printing areas so that ink from the ink roller sticks only to the printing areas of the image. The ink is then transferred to another, intermediate roller bearing a rubber blanket. This presses the ink onto the paper. 'Offset' refers to the transfer of the inked image to an intermediate roller.

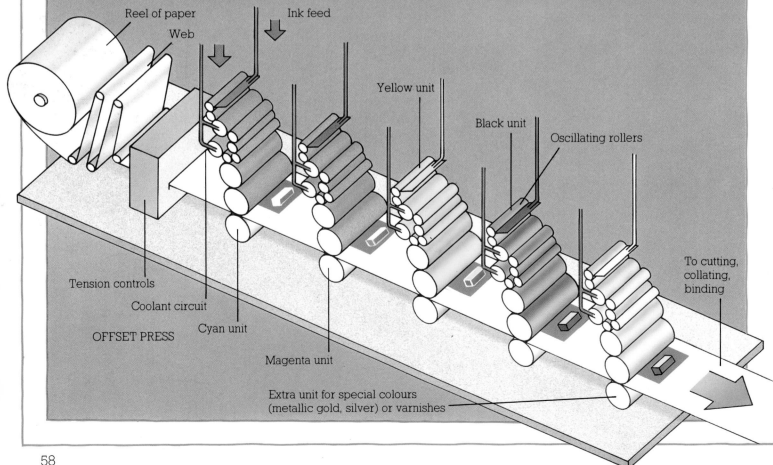

Reel of paper

Web

Ink feed

Yellow unit

Black unit

Oscillating rollers

Tension controls

Coolant circuit

Cyan unit

OFFSET PRESS

Magenta unit

To cutting, collating, binding

Extra unit for special colours (metallic gold, silver) or varnishes

6 PHOTOCOPIER

This fairly recent method of copy-printing is suitable for a few tens or perhaps hundreds of copies. But it becomes expensive for larger numbers, compared to other printing processes. Photocopying is based on the principle that static electricity attracts objects. This happens when you rub a balloon on a dry woollen jumper. The friction of rubbing generates static electricity that makes the balloon 'stick' to the jumper. The photocopier has a large electrostatic drum that is charged with static electricity. The image to be copied is beamed down from the platen onto the drum by a series of mirrors and lenses. It removes the charges in some areas. The charged parts attract the toner powder. This is transferred to a sheet of paper and then made permanent, usually by heat.

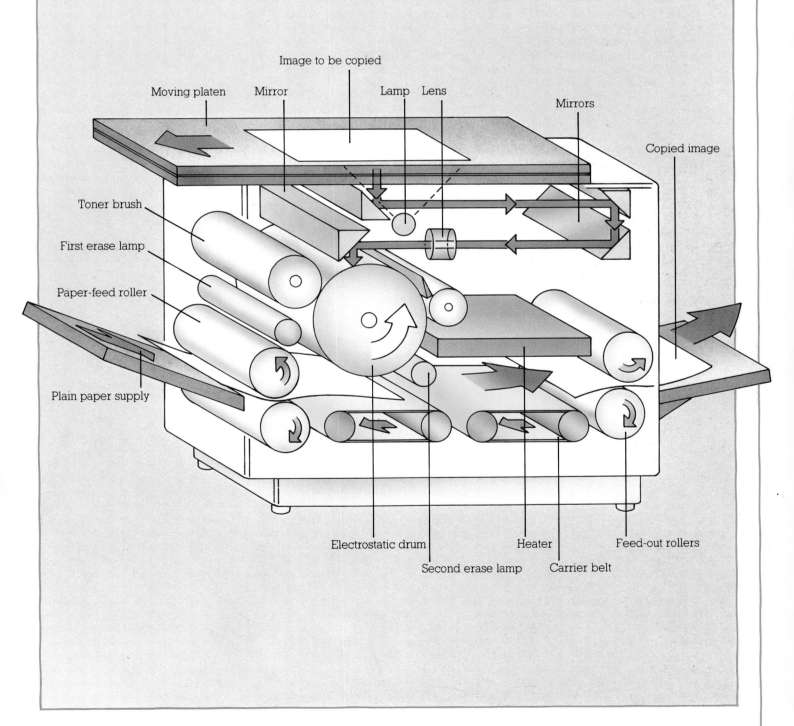

Image to be copied

Moving platen   Mirror   Lamp Lens   Mirrors

Copied image

Toner brush

First erase lamp

Paper-feed roller

Plain paper supply

Electrostatic drum   Heater   Feed-out rollers

Second erase lamp   Carrier belt

THE TELEVISION STUDIO

SATELLITE TELEVISION 5
RHEOSTAT 3
ANIMATION 4
TELEVISION CAMERA 2
AUTOCUE 1

1 AUTOCUE

Imagine being in a brightly lit room when it is almost dark outside. Look at the window. You can see both the scene outside, through the glass, and the things inside the room, reflected in the glass. The autocue machine works along the same lines. There is a glass sheet between the newsreader and the screen. The camera 'sees' the newsreader through the glass The newsreader sees the camera – and also the reflections of the words on the monitor screen. As the newsreader reads the words, the text scrolls (moves) up the screen.

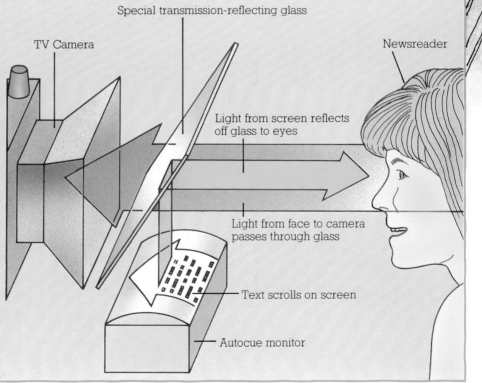

TV Camera

Special transmission-reflecting glass

Newsreader

Light from screen reflects off glass to eyes

Light from face to camera passes through glass

Text scrolls on screen

Autocue monitor

2

TELEVISION CAMERA

White light is made up of a mixture of different colours, which can be separated by a prism to form the colours of the spectrum. The prism in one type of television camera is designed to split light from the scene into three colours: red, green and blue. It does this by *refraction*. Each colour of light consists of rays of a slightly different wavelength. The different wavelengths are refracted by slightly different amounts as they pass into and out of the glass of the prism.

The angles of the prism's faces are arranged so that the three main colours are separated from each other and shone out of the prism in different directions. Each colour is beamed into a detector that scans the image and converts the patterns of light rays into electrical signals. In the television set, the three colours are recombined on the screen (page 75). The latest television cameras use a single electronic light detector instead of three separate tubes.

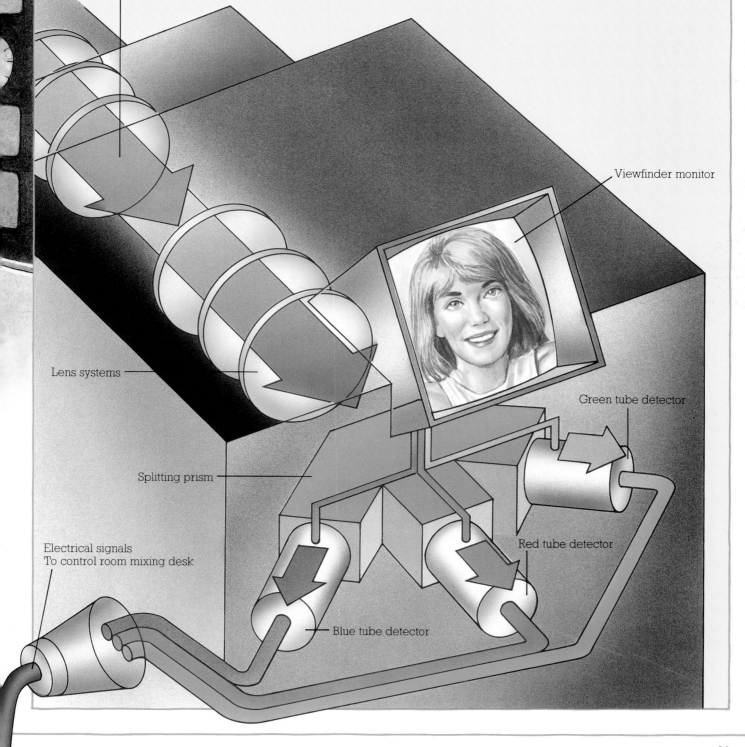

LIGHT RAYS FROM IMAGE

Viewfinder monitor

Lens systems

Green tube detector

Splitting prism

Red tube detector

Electrical signals
To control room mixing desk

Blue tube detector

3 RHEOSTAT

Many of the knobs and sliders on electrical equipment operate rheostats. The basic rheostat is a coil of resistance wire, touched by a sliding contact on one side, which forms part of an electrical circuit. When the electricity passes through only a few turns of the coil, it meets only a slight resistance. If the contact is slid to the other end, there is much more resistance wire included in the circuit, and the electricity is thereby reduced. A similar device works by turning a metal wiper around an arc-shaped resistance bar to 'tap off' varying amounts of electricity.

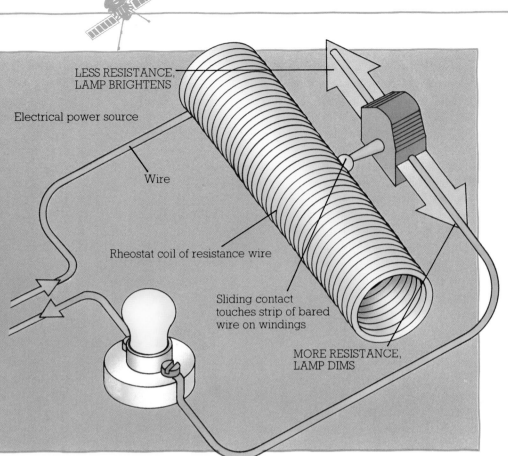

LESS RESISTANCE, LAMP BRIGHTENS

Electrical power source

Wire

Rheostat coil of resistance wire

Sliding contact touches strip of bared wire on windings

MORE RESISTANCE, LAMP DIMS

4 ANIMATION

A television or cinema screen does not show a continuously moving image. It shows a number of still images in rapid succession, many each second. The eye blurs together these quickly-changing still images and sees them as a 'moving picture'. Animation is the technique of making a 'moving picture' from a series of still images created by artists, or by models, or photographs, or computerized graphics. Cartoons are one familiar example. Each image, or frame, is drawn and coloured as a separate piece of artwork. These are recorded one by one, as individual frames on cine film or videotape (pages 76, 83). When played back at normal speed, the frames blur together and create the illusion of movement.

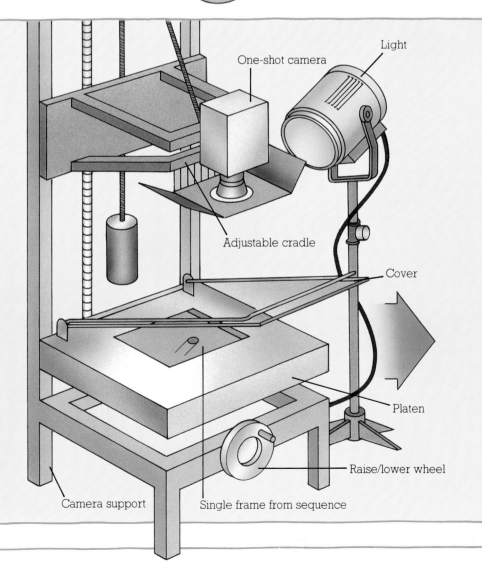

Light

One-shot camera

Adjustable cradle

Cover

Platen

Raise/lower wheel

Camera support

Single frame from sequence

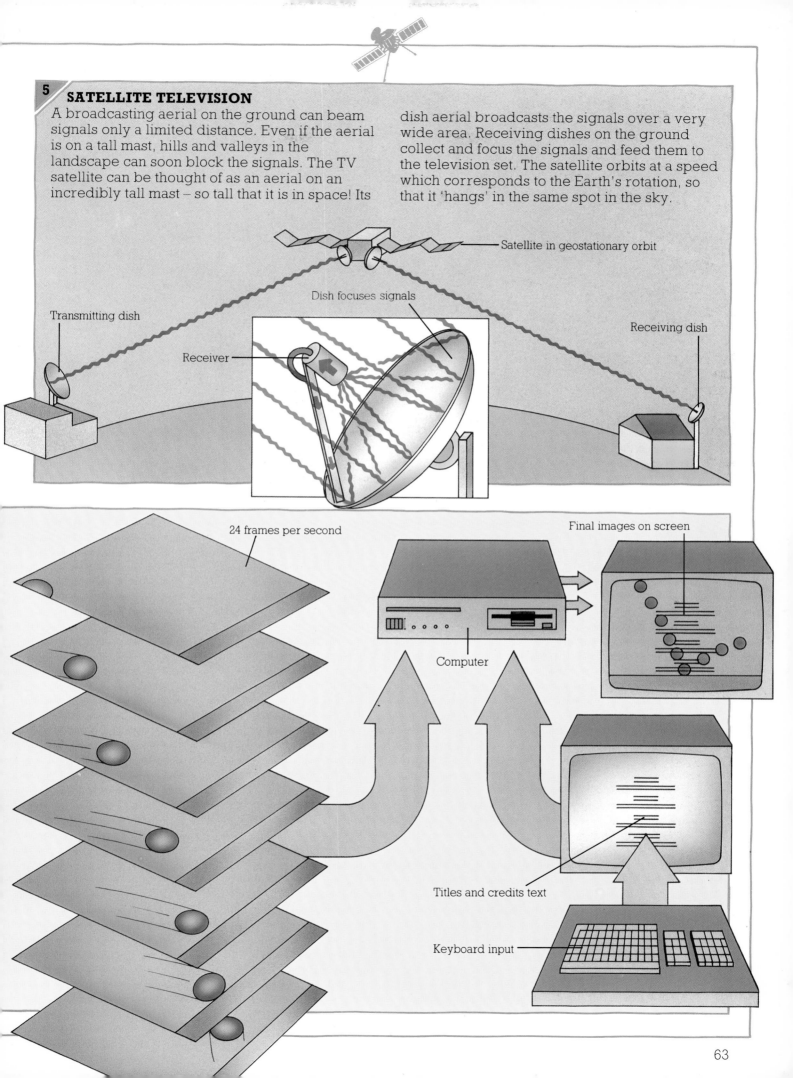

5 SATELLITE TELEVISION

A broadcasting aerial on the ground can beam signals only a limited distance. Even if the aerial is on a tall mast, hills and valleys in the landscape can soon block the signals. The TV satellite can be thought of as an aerial on an incredibly tall mast – so tall that it is in space! Its dish aerial broadcasts the signals over a very wide area. Receiving dishes on the ground collect and focus the signals and feed them to the television set. The satellite orbits at a speed which corresponds to the Earth's rotation, so that it 'hangs' in the same spot in the sky.

Satellite in geostationary orbit

Dish focuses signals

Transmitting dish

Receiver

Receiving dish

24 frames per second

Final images on screen

Computer

Titles and credits text

Keyboard input

GRAND PRIX CIRCUIT

SUSPENSION, STEERING AND BRAKES 2

RACING CAR 1

PETROL ENGINE 3

DIFFERENTIAL 6

CLUTCH A GEARBOX 4

ENGINE LAYOUTS 5

1 RACING CAR

Formula One racing cars are at the forefront of automobile design and technology. Even with engines limited to a capacity of 3500 ccs (cubic centimetres), they produce up to 10 times the power of a standard family car engine of about 1400 ccs (1.4 litres). At speeds of 300 kilometres per hour on the track's straight, aerodynamic design is very important. Air passing over the wings creates downwards thrust. This presses the car down, keeping its tyres firmly in contact with the track, to minimize wheel spins and skids. The driver 'sits' in an almost lying position, for extra streamlining.

Air intake

Rear wing

Disc brakes

Gearbox

Engine

Cooling radiators

SUSPENSION, BRAKES AND STEERING

The car's suspension system helps to absorb bumps and hollows in the road, giving a smoother ride. It also allows the car body to tilt slightly as it goes round a bend, for better cornering. A typical suspension unit has both a coil spring and a hydraulic damper unit. The spring absorbs the bumps and hollows, and the damper stops the spring from bouncing. Formula One cars and other performance cars have disc brakes. Stationary brake pads attached to the chassis press on a disc that revolves with the roadwheel. The disc brake is more effective and stays cooler than the drum brake, in which curved brake shoes press outwards onto the inside of a revolving drum attached to the roadwheel. Both types work by hydraulic pressure (page 42). In rack-and-pinion steering, the steering wheel turns a shaft that ends in a small pinion gear. This meshes with the rack, which is a 'straightened' gear wheel. As the pinion rotates the rack slides along, moving levers that turn the roadwheels.

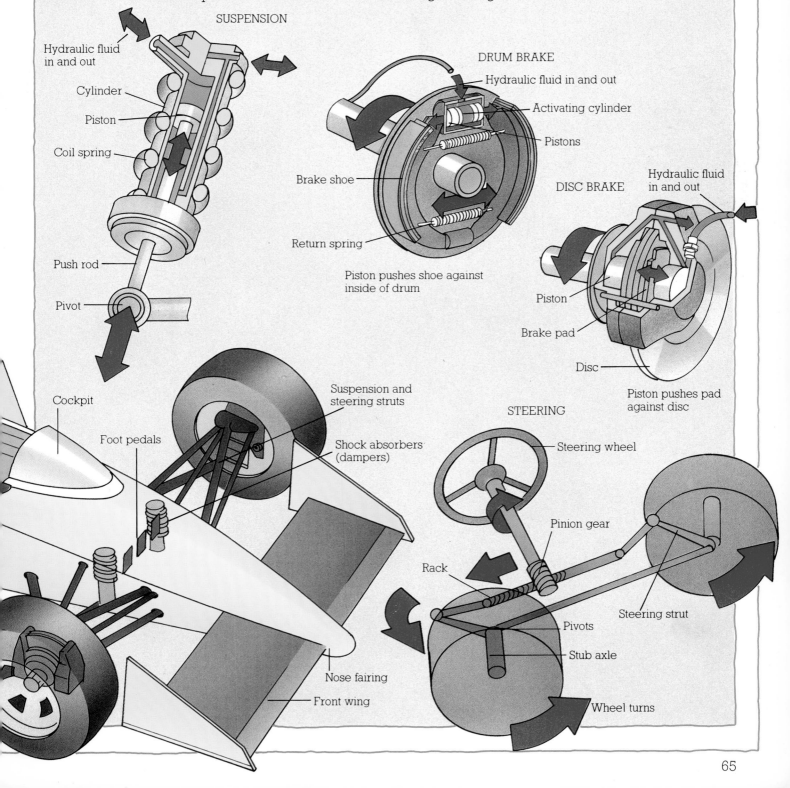

SUSPENSION

Hydraulic fluid in and out

Cylinder

Piston

Coil spring

Push rod

Pivot

DRUM BRAKE

Hydraulic fluid in and out

Activating cylinder

Pistons

Brake shoe

Return spring

Piston pushes shoe against inside of drum

DISC BRAKE

Hydraulic fluid in and out

Piston

Brake pad

Disc

Piston pushes pad against disc

Cockpit

Foot pedals

Suspension and steering struts

Shock absorbers (dampers)

STEERING

Steering wheel

Pinion gear

Rack

Pivots

Steering strut

Stub axle

Nose fairing

Front wing

Wheel turns

3

PETROL ENGINE

In the type of internal combustion engine that runs on petrol the energy comes from chemical substances in the petrol, which has been purified from crude petroleum (page 101). Inside each cylinder of the engine, a mixture of petrol vapour and air is ignited by an electrically-produced spark (*opposite*). This produces a mini-explosion, or combustion, which forces the piston down inside the cylinder. The piston is linked to a crankshaft that transforms an oscillating (to-and-fro) movement into a rotary one. Most ordinary car engines have four or six cylinders. As each piston moves inside its cylinder, from its lowest to its highest position, it pushes or *displaces* a certain volume of air from the cylinder. Add together these displacement volumes for all the cylinders in the engine, and this gives the capacity for the engine, usually measured in cubic centimetres (ccs). If each piston in a four-cylinder engine displaces 500 ccs, then the capacity of the engine is $4 \times 500 = 2000$ ccs (two litres).

The carburettor mixes air with fuel to give the correct explosive mixture for the cylinder. Each piston on its *induction* stroke (*opposite*) sucks in air from the atmosphere. The air flows through a narrowed part of the carburettor, the *venturi*, where it speeds up and sucks in fuel from the fuel pipe. A tapered needle moves up or down inside a tube to control the amount of fuel entering the carburettor.

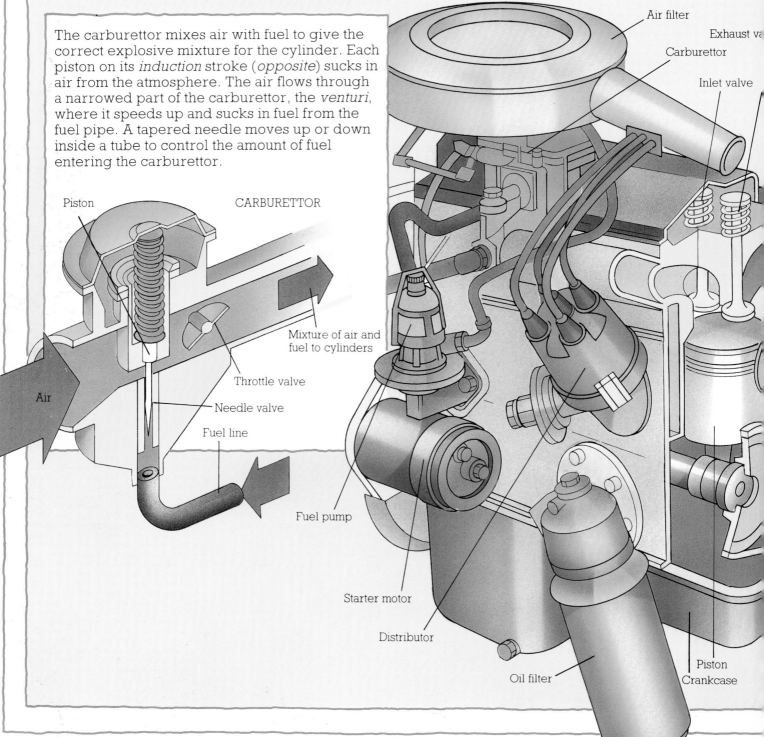

Piston

CARBURETTOR

Mixture of air and fuel to cylinders

Throttle valve

Needle valve

Fuel line

Air

Air filter

Exhaust va

Carburettor

Inlet valve

Fuel pump

Starter motor

Distributor

Oil filter

Piston

Crankcase

After combustion, exhaust gases rushing from the cylinder represent energy going to waste. The turbocharger is a turbine-based device that uses these waste gases to make the engine more powerful. It forces extra air and fuel into the cylinders, which increases the power from each 'explosion'.

In the diesel type of internal combustion engine the extremely high pressure inside the cylinder raises the temperature of the air/fuel mixture to exploding point. In a petrol engine, a spark plug makes an electrically-generated spark which 'sets fire' to the mixture. As the engine turns, valves in the top of the cylinder open and close. These work in the correct sequence to let in the air/fuel mixture, contain it during combustion, and then let out the waste gases afterwards.

The family car's petrol engine is four-stroke. Each piston repeatedly goes through a cycle that lasts four strokes: down, up, down, up. First is the down stroke of *induction*, when air/fuel mixture is drawn into the cylinder. Second is *compression*, as the mixture is squeezed, so raising its temperature. Third is *ignition*, when the mixture is exploded by a spark. Fourth is *exhaust*, as waste gases from the explosion are pushed out. Some smaller engines are two-stroke (*right, below*).

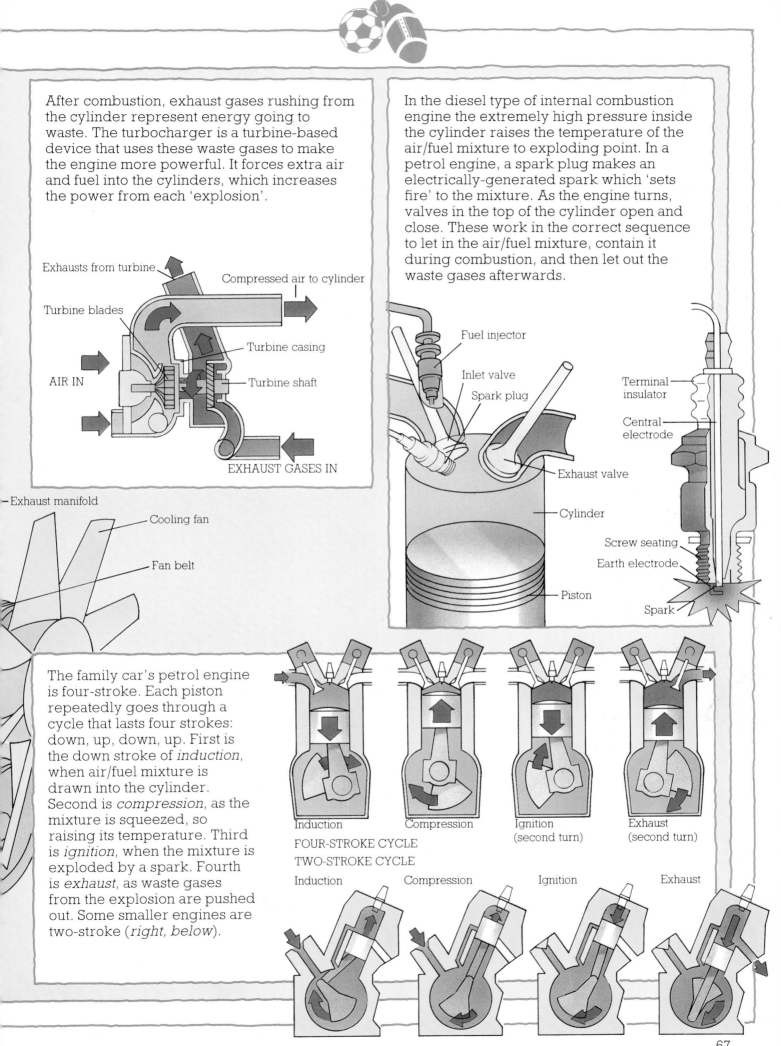

Exhausts from turbine

Compressed air to cylinder

Turbine blades

Turbine casing

AIR IN

Turbine shaft

EXHAUST GASES IN

Exhaust manifold

Cooling fan

Fan belt

Fuel injector

Inlet valve

Spark plug

Exhaust valve

Cylinder

Piston

Terminal insulator

Central electrode

Screw seating

Earth electrode

Spark

Induction · Compression · Ignition (second turn) · Exhaust (second turn)

FOUR-STROKE CYCLE

TWO-STROKE CYCLE

Induction · Compression · Ignition · Exhaust

4

CLUTCH AND GEARBOX

There are at least four mechanical devices involved in changing the turning motion of the car's engine to its roadwheels: clutch, gearbox, propeller shaft and final drives. Together, these are called the transmission.

All the time the engine is running, the crankshaft is turning – but the car may be standing still in neutral, or cruising along in top gear. The clutch disconnects the engine's spinning crankshaft from the gearbox when changing gear. When the clutch is engaged or 'in' (pedal up), the plates press together and transfer the turning motion to the gearbox. The clutch is disengaged or put 'out' (pedal pressed) when the two plates are pulled slightly apart. Inside the gearbox, a system of shafts and gear wheels slide to and fro to change gear. In first gear, the engine turns the roadwheels slowly but with much *torque* (turning force). In top gear, for the same engine speed, the roadwheels turn much faster but with less torque.

Some cars have automatic transmission (*bottom*), where the gears change themselves according to the speed of the engine and the turning power needed.

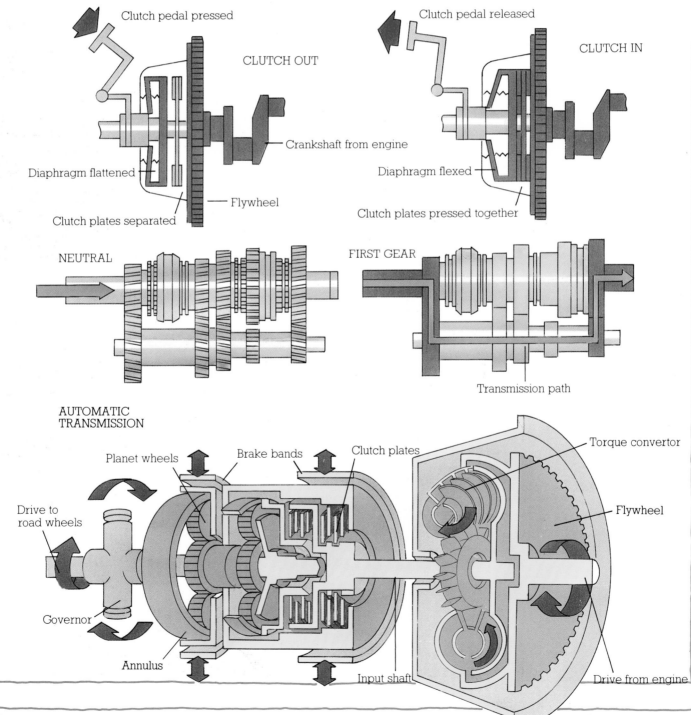

Clutch pedal pressed

CLUTCH OUT

Crankshaft from engine

Diaphragm flattened

Flywheel

Clutch plates separated

Clutch pedal released

CLUTCH IN

Diaphragm flexed

Clutch plates pressed together

NEUTRAL

FIRST GEAR

Transmission path

AUTOMATIC TRANSMISSION

Planet wheels

Brake bands

Clutch plates

Torque convertor

Drive to road wheels

Flywheel

Governor

Annulus

Input shaft

Drive from engine

5   ENGINE LAYOUTS

A car's stability, handling and manoeuvrability depend partly on how the weight of the various parts is spread between the four roadwheels. Particularly important is the position of the heaviest component, the engine. Also important is whether the engine drives the front or rear wheels, or all four wheels together. A Formula One racing car has a mid-mounted, in-line engine that drives the rear wheels. Several other layouts or *configurations*, are shown here. The mid-engined layout provides good weight distribution. However, in a family car the engine would take up much of the space that is normally set aside for rear passengers and luggage. Four-wheel drive is best for soft, bumpy or otherwise difficult terrain.

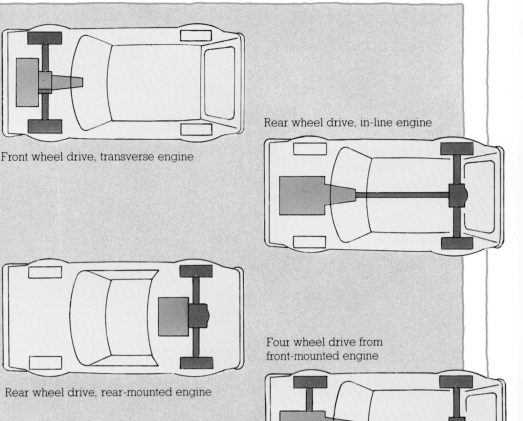

Front wheel drive, transverse engine

Rear wheel drive, in-line engine

Rear wheel drive, rear-mounted engine

Four wheel drive from front-mounted engine

6   DIFFERENTIAL

As a car rounds a corner, the wheels on the outside of the bend travel farther than those on the inside (*far right*). If the wheels are not driven by the engine, each can rotate independently at its own speed. But wheels driven by the engine would skip and skid if they rotated at the same speed. The differential lets the roadwheels turn at different speeds. The propellor shaft transmits power to the crown wheel. This turns two *bevel* gears, which mesh with bevel gears on the half-shafts. When the inner roadwheel slows down, the outer one speeds up and the bevel gears attached to the crown wheel turn to take up the difference.

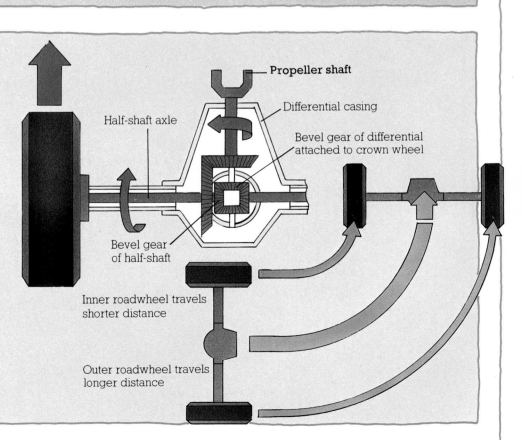

Propeller shaft

Differential casing

Half-shaft axle

Bevel gear of differential attached to crown wheel

Bevel gear of half-shaft

Inner roadwheel travels shorter distance

Outer roadwheel travels longer distance

THE SPORTS CENTRE

SAILING 6

SOCCER BALL 5

BOUNCING 8

SHOOTING 7

BAR CODE 3

TURNSTILE 2

LCD STOPWATCH 4

LIGHT METER 1

1 LIGHT METER

In outdoor games such as tennis and cricket, players should be able to see the ball clearly! When the sky is overcast, or towards dusk, the light may be too dim for good play. In the light meter, a photo-resistor changes its resistance to electricity according to how much light falls on it. The result is shown by a small needle and dial or a liquid crystal display (LCD).

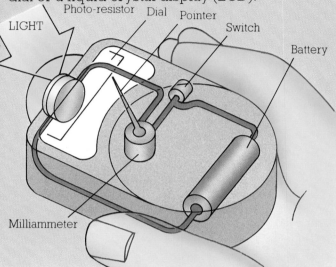

Photo-resistor   Dial   Pointer
LIGHT   Switch
                                Battery

Milliammeter

2 TURNSTILE

This simple, robust machine is a ratchet. The teeth on the cog wheel slope in one direction. The wheel can turn one way, since the single tooth or 'dog' on the sprung bar is pushed aside smoothly by the sloping part of each tooth on the wheel. But try to turn the wheel the other way, and the dog jams against the first tooth and prevents the wheel rotating.

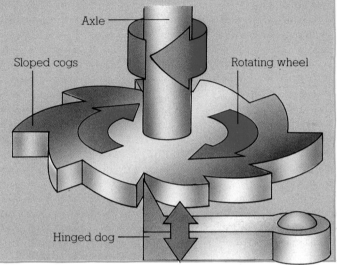

Axle
Sloped cogs   Rotating wheel

Hinged dog

3 BAR CODE

Many items are now labelled with a bar code, a series of thick and thin black lines. They carry encoded information – from the membership number of a sports club, to the price and stock number of a packet of washing powder in a supermarket. The code is scanned by a beam, which turns light pulses into electrical signals that are fed into a computer for processing.

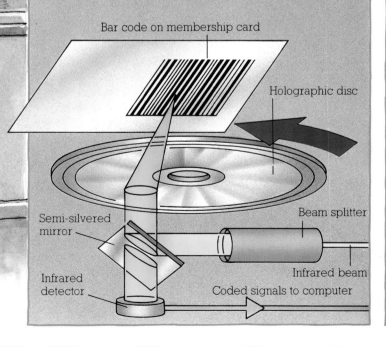

Bar code on membership card

Holographic disc

Semi-silvered mirror

Beam splitter

Infrared detector
Infrared beam
Coded signals to computer

4 LCD STOPWATCH

Each segment of a Liquid Crystal Display consists of many liquid crystals sandwiched between two electrodes. The crystals can move or 'flow' like a liquid. When electricity passes between the electrodes, it twists the crystals so that they do not transmit polarized light; that segment then appears black. Place the lenses of two polarized sunglasses together and twist them, for the same effect.

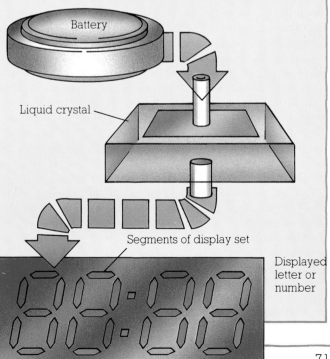

Battery

Liquid crystal

Segments of display set

Displayed letter or number

5   SOCCER BALL

An old-fashioned soccer ball has leather panels stitched together to leave a slit-like opening for the inflatable bladder inside. The opening is then laced up like a shoe. However this causes problems because of unequal weight distribution, which makes the ball wobble as it spins. It can also be uncomfortable for a player who heads the ball on the laced-up part! Most balls today have leather panels that are shaped in groups to form parts of a sphere. They are stitched together inside out. Before the last seam is sewn, the ball is turned 'inside in' and the inflatable bladder is inserted. The finished ball is perfectly round and well-balanced.

6   SAILS AND SAILING

Sail-based sports such as yachting and windsurfing rely on the energy of the wind to push on the broad surface of the sail, which is attached to the craft. Being blown along in the direction of the wind is known as *running* (*near right*). In order to travel across the wind, the craft and sail are set at angles as shown for *reaching* (*far right*). The resistance of the craft to being pushed sideways combines with the direction of the wind on the sail, to make the craft travel forwards. The sailor can move into the wind by *beating*, to the left and right alternately, on a zig-zag course into the wind (*middle right*).

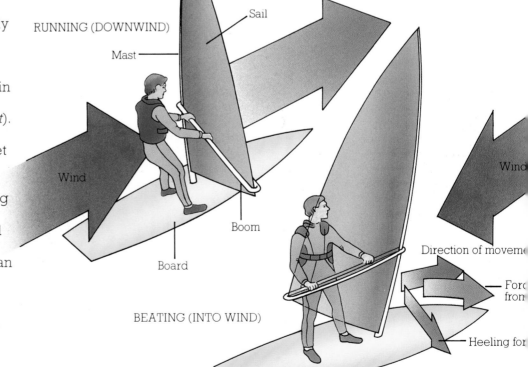

RUNNING (DOWNWIND)

Direction of movement

Sail

Mast

Wind

Boom

Board

BEATING (INTO WIND)

Wind

Direction of moveme[nt]

Heeling for[ce]

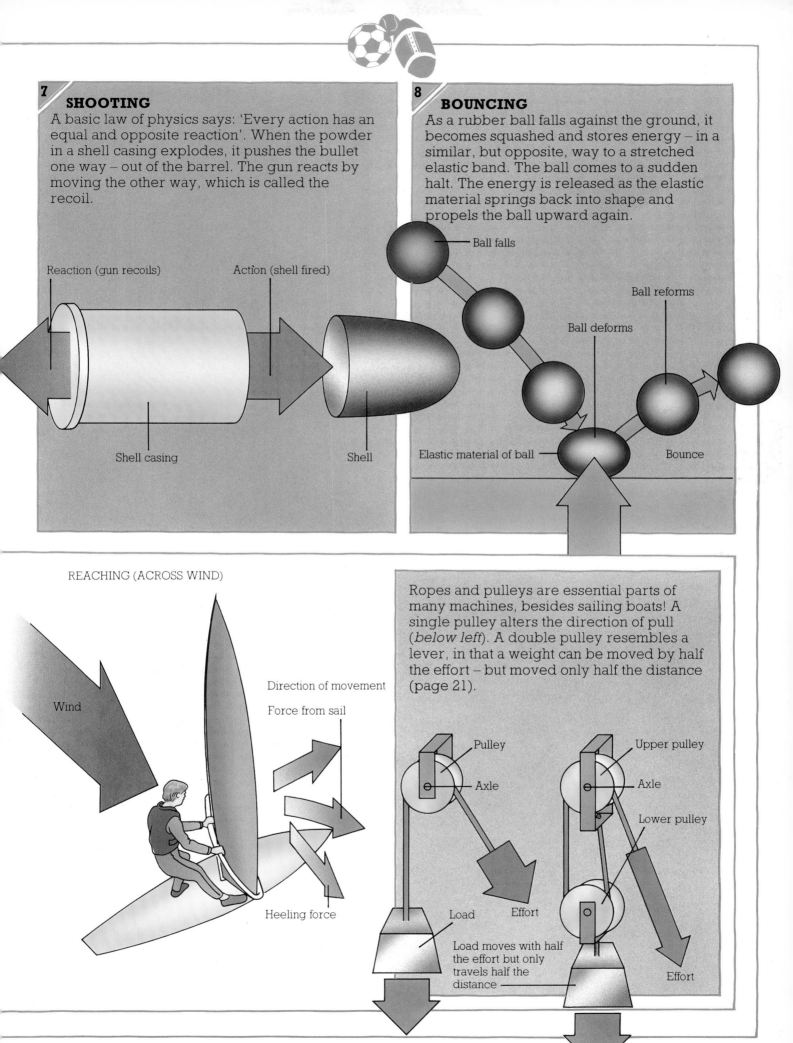

7 SHOOTING

A basic law of physics says: 'Every action has an equal and opposite reaction'. When the powder in a shell casing explodes, it pushes the bullet one way – out of the barrel. The gun reacts by moving the other way, which is called the recoil.

Reaction (gun recoils)

Action (shell fired)

Shell casing

Shell

8 BOUNCING

As a rubber ball falls against the ground, it becomes squashed and stores energy – in a similar, but opposite, way to a stretched elastic band. The ball comes to a sudden halt. The energy is released as the elastic material springs back into shape and propels the ball upward again.

Ball falls

Ball reforms

Ball deforms

Elastic material of ball

Bounce

REACHING (ACROSS WIND)

Wind

Direction of movement

Force from sail

Heeling force

Ropes and pulleys are essential parts of many machines, besides sailing boats! A single pulley alters the direction of pull (*below left*). A double pulley resembles a lever, in that a weight can be moved by half the effort – but moved only half the distance (page 21).

Pulley

Axle

Load

Effort

Upper pulley

Axle

Lower pulley

Load moves with half the effort but only travels half the distance

Effort

ENTERTAINMENT

TELEVISION

VIDEO CAMERA AND PLAYER

HI-FI MUSIC SYSTEM

PIANO

1 PIANO

Each piano key works as a simple lever that sets in motion a series of levers, catches and springs. The result is that the damper lifts from the string as the hammer strikes it. As long as the key is held down, the damper stays away from the string. When the key is allowed to return, the damper comes back into contact with the string and stops its vibrations. A foot pedal moves all the dampers so that the strings continue to ring even after the keys return.

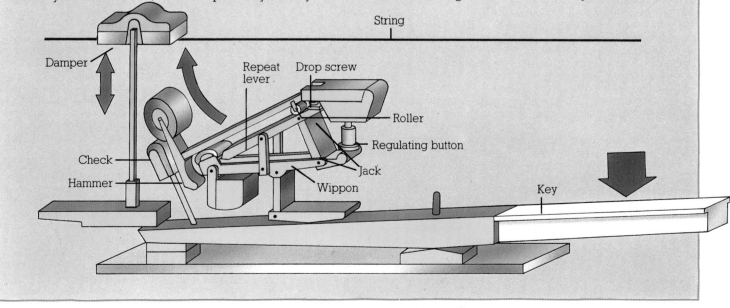

Damper

String

Repeat lever

Drop screw

Roller

Regulating button

Jack

Check

Hammer

Wippon

Key

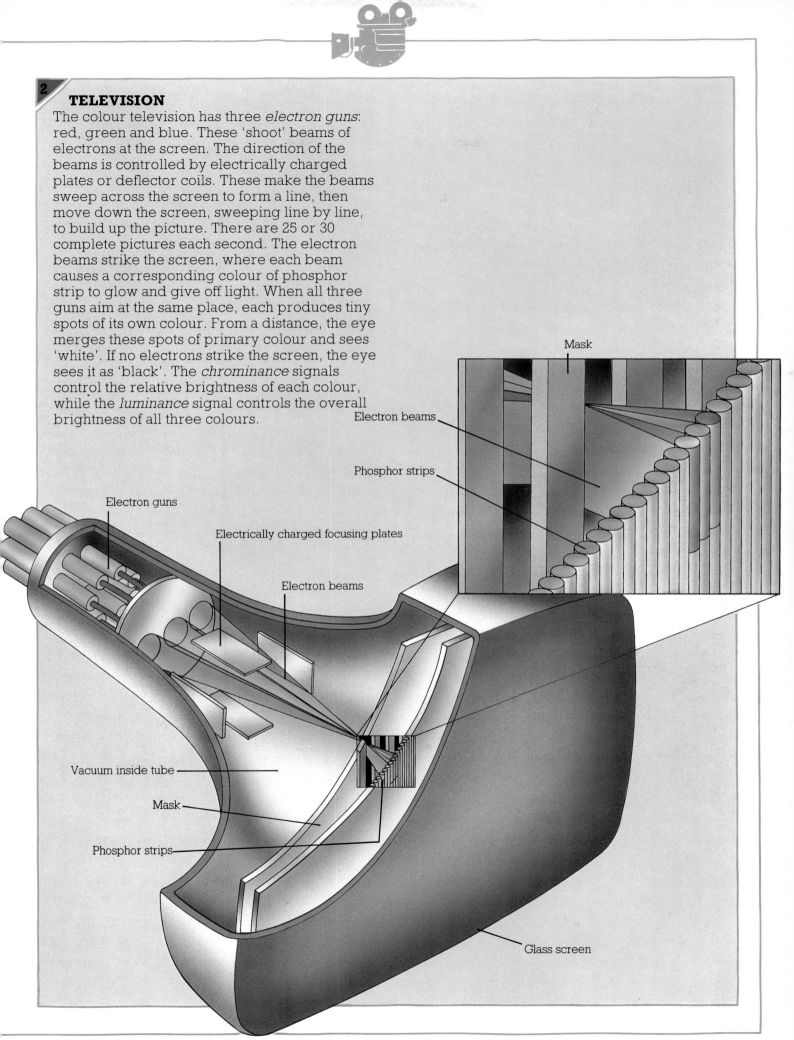

TELEVISION

The colour television has three *electron guns*: red, green and blue. These 'shoot' beams of electrons at the screen. The direction of the beams is controlled by electrically charged plates or deflector coils. These make the beams sweep across the screen to form a line, then move down the screen, sweeping line by line, to build up the picture. There are 25 or 30 complete pictures each second. The electron beams strike the screen, where each beam causes a corresponding colour of phosphor strip to glow and give off light. When all three guns aim at the same place, each produces tiny spots of its own colour. From a distance, the eye merges these spots of primary colour and sees 'white'. If no electrons strike the screen, the eye sees it as 'black'. The *chrominance* signals control the relative brightness of each colour, while the *luminance* signal controls the overall brightness of all three colours.

Mask

Electron beams

Phosphor strips

Electron guns

Electrically charged focusing plates

Electron beams

Vacuum inside tube

Mask

Phosphor strips

Glass screen

CAMCORDER

A camcorder does not use light to create a chemical change in photographic film, as in the ordinary camera (page 55). Instead, the light is focused onto a target plate that has a layer of *photoconductive* material. This is a material that conducts varying amounts of electricity, according to the amount and colour of light that shines onto it. The photoconductive material is scanned point-by-point across the plate by electronic circuitry, and the image on it is coded into a stream of electrical signals. These are recorded as tiny magnetized patches on magnetic tape – dozens of images each second. The tape is contained in a plastic case called a videocassette. When the tape is played, the record-playback heads pick up the coded patches of magnetism and convert them into electrical signals, which are fed to the television set. Sound is also recorded on the tape.

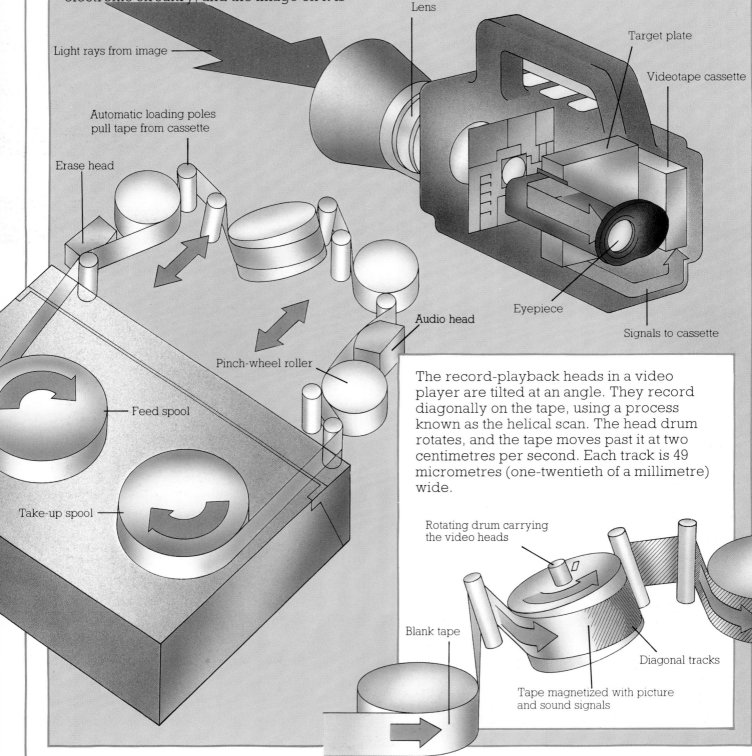

Light rays from image

Automatic loading poles pull tape from cassette

Erase head

Lens

Target plate

Videotape cassette

Eyepiece

Signals to cassette

Audio head

Pinch-wheel roller

Feed spool

Take-up spool

The record-playback heads in a video player are tilted at an angle. They record diagonally on the tape, using a process known as the helical scan. The head drum rotates, and the tape moves past it at two centimetres per second. Each track is 49 micrometres (one-twentieth of a millimetre) wide.

Rotating drum carrying the video heads

Blank tape

Diagonal tracks

Tape magnetized with picture and sound signals

HI-FI MUSIC SYSTEM

A typical home hi-fi (high-fidelity) system consists of inputs, an amplifier and a control unit, and outputs. The inputs detect coded signals in a variety of forms, turn them into electrical signals, and feed them to the amplifier. For example, the radio tuner detects signals broadcast as radio waves, using its aerial. In the vinyl disc 'record player', the signals are coded as bumps and waves in a V-shaped groove. In a compact disc player, they are in the form of microscopic bumps and pits which are read by a laser beam. In an audio cassette, the signals are tiny patches of magnetism on the tape. The signals are altered by the tone controls, made stronger in the amplifier, and then fed to the outputs – usually loudspeakers or headphones.

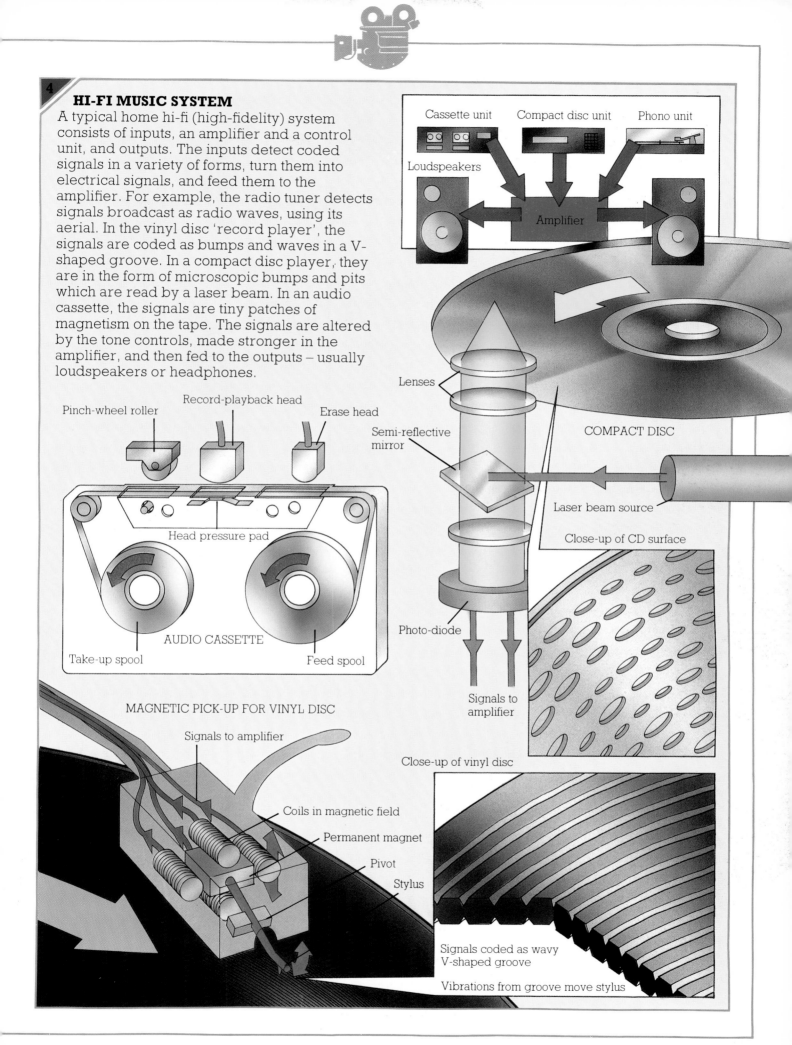

Cassette unit   Compact disc unit   Phono unit

Loudspeakers

Amplifier

COMPACT DISC

Lenses

Semi-reflective mirror

Laser beam source

Close-up of CD surface

Photo-diode

Signals to amplifier

Pinch-wheel roller

Record-playback head

Erase head

Head pressure pad

AUDIO CASSETTE

Take-up spool

Feed spool

MAGNETIC PICK-UP FOR VINYL DISC

Signals to amplifier

Coils in magnetic field

Permanent magnet

Pivot

Stylus

Close-up of vinyl disc

Signals coded as wavy V-shaped groove

Vibrations from groove move stylus

ROCK CONCERT

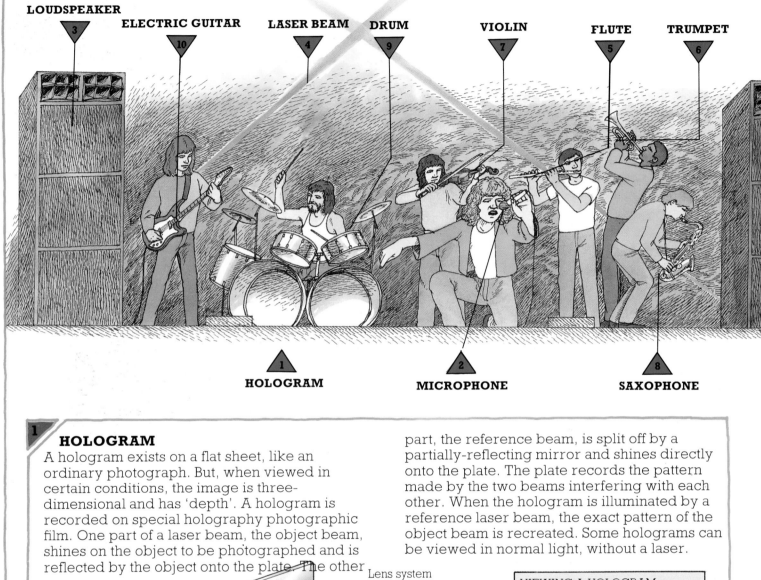

LOUDSPEAKER ▼ 3

ELECTRIC GUITAR ▼ 10

LASER BEAM ▼ 4

DRUM ▼ 9

VIOLIN ▼ 7

FLUTE ▼ 5

TRUMPET ▼ 6

▲ 1 HOLOGRAM

▲ 2 MICROPHONE

▲ 8 SAXOPHONE

1 HOLOGRAM

A hologram exists on a flat sheet, like an ordinary photograph. But, when viewed in certain conditions, the image is three-dimensional and has 'depth'. A hologram is recorded on special holography photographic film. One part of a laser beam, the object beam, shines on the object to be photographed and is reflected by the object onto the plate. The other part, the reference beam, is split off by a partially-reflecting mirror and shines directly onto the plate. The plate records the pattern made by the two beams interfering with each other. When the hologram is illuminated by a reference laser beam, the exact pattern of the object beam is recreated. Some holograms can be viewed in normal light, without a laser.

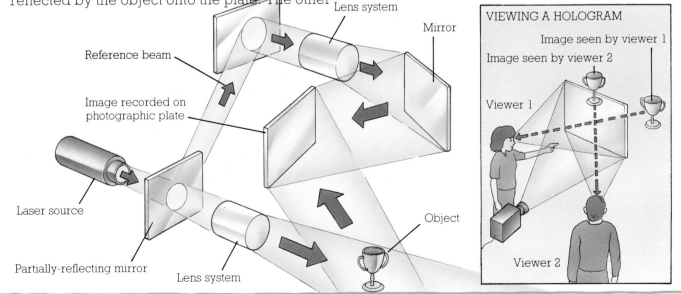

Reference beam

Image recorded on photographic plate

Laser source

Partially-reflecting mirror

Lens system

Lens system

Mirror

Object

VIEWING A HOLOGRAM

Image seen by viewer 1

Image seen by viewer 2

Viewer 1

Viewer 2

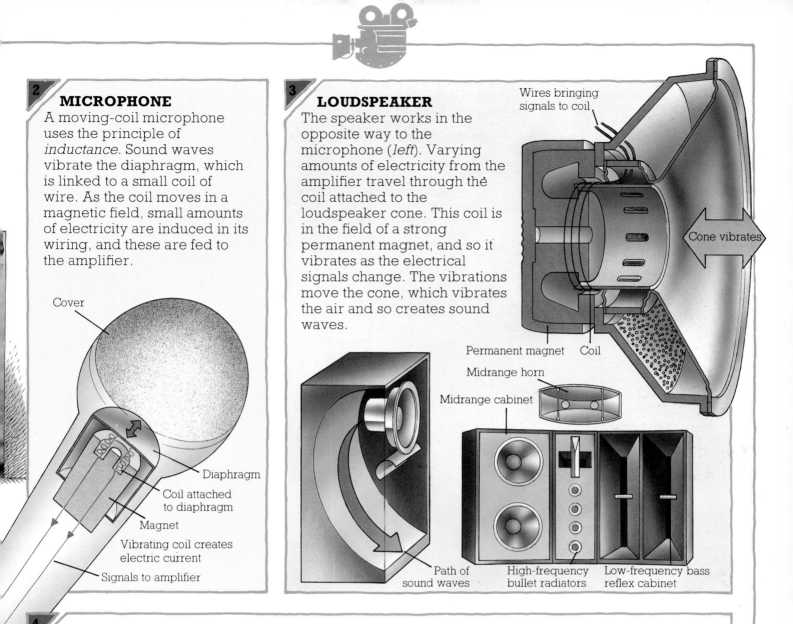

2 MICROPHONE

A moving-coil microphone uses the principle of *inductance*. Sound waves vibrate the diaphragm, which is linked to a small coil of wire. As the coil moves in a magnetic field, small amounts of electricity are induced in its wiring, and these are fed to the amplifier.

Cover

Diaphragm

Coil attached to diaphragm

Magnet

Vibrating coil creates electric current

Signals to amplifier

3 LOUDSPEAKER

The speaker works in the opposite way to the microphone (*left*). Varying amounts of electricity from the amplifier travel through the coil attached to the loudspeaker cone. This coil is in the field of a strong permanent magnet, and so it vibrates as the electrical signals change. The vibrations move the cone, which vibrates the air and so creates sound waves.

Wires bringing signals to coil

Cone vibrates

Permanent magnet   Coil

Midrange horn

Midrange cabinet

Path of sound waves

High-frequency bullet radiators

Low-frequency bass reflex cabinet

4 LASER

High-voltage electricity passes through a glass tube containing a mixture of gases, such as helium and neon. The electricity stimulates the gas atoms to give off tiny 'packets' of light, called photons. These stimulate other atoms to emit photons. Mirrors reflect most of the light back into the gas for further amplification. A partially silvered mirror at one end allows out a narrow, parallel beam of intensely bright, pure, single-colour light – the laser beam. 'Laser' stands for Light Amplification by Stimulated Emission of Radiation.

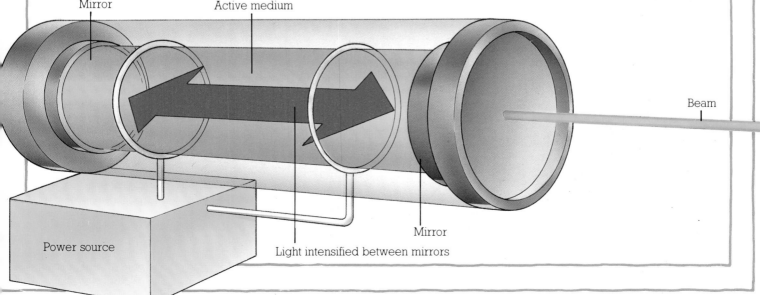

Mirror

Active medium

Beam

Mirror

Light intensified between mirrors

Power source

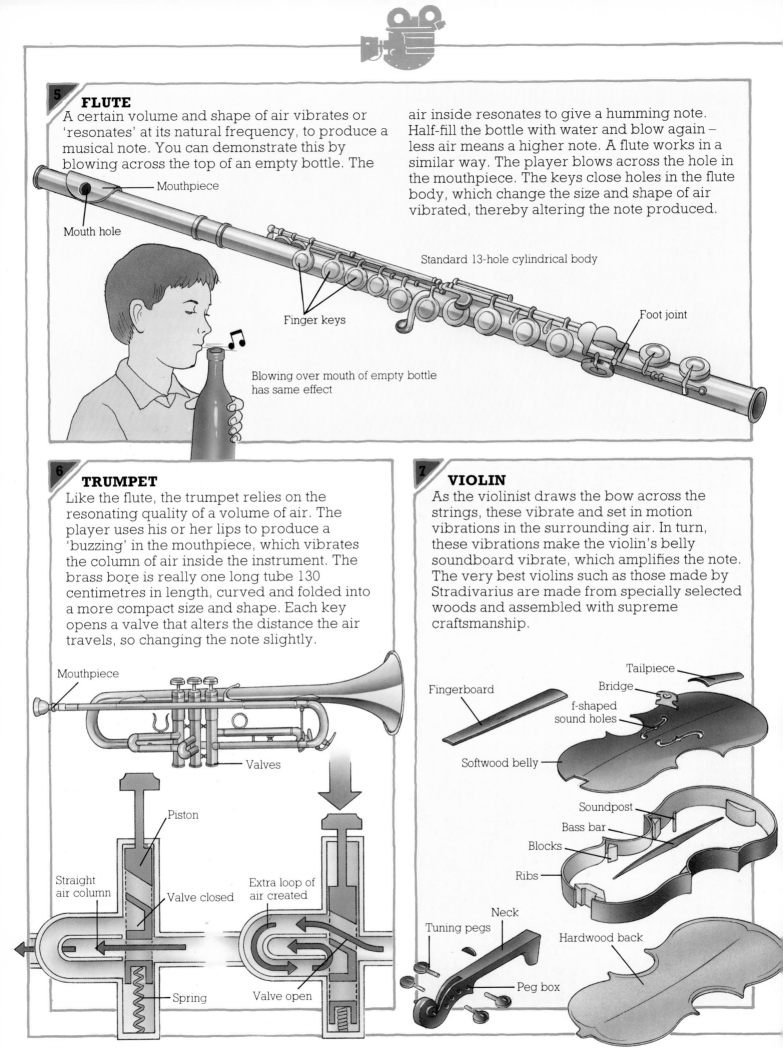

5 FLUTE

A certain volume and shape of air vibrates or 'resonates' at its natural frequency, to produce a musical note. You can demonstrate this by blowing across the top of an empty bottle. The air inside resonates to give a humming note. Half-fill the bottle with water and blow again – less air means a higher note. A flute works in a similar way. The player blows across the hole in the mouthpiece. The keys close holes in the flute body, which change the size and shape of air vibrated, thereby altering the note produced.

Mouthpiece

Mouth hole

Finger keys

Standard 13-hole cylindrical body

Foot joint

Blowing over mouth of empty bottle has same effect

6 TRUMPET

Like the flute, the trumpet relies on the resonating quality of a volume of air. The player uses his or her lips to produce a 'buzzing' in the mouthpiece, which vibrates the column of air inside the instrument. The brass bore is really one long tube 130 centimetres in length, curved and folded into a more compact size and shape. Each key opens a valve that alters the distance the air travels, so changing the note slightly.

Mouthpiece

Valves

Piston

Straight air column

Valve closed

Extra loop of air created

Valve open

Spring

7 VIOLIN

As the violinist draws the bow across the strings, these vibrate and set in motion vibrations in the surrounding air. In turn, these vibrations make the violin's belly soundboard vibrate, which amplifies the note. The very best violins such as those made by Stradivarius are made from specially selected woods and assembled with supreme craftsmanship.

Fingerboard

Tailpiece

Bridge

f-shaped sound holes

Softwood belly

Soundpost

Bass bar

Blocks

Ribs

Neck

Tuning pegs

Hardwood back

Peg box

8 SAXOPHONE

This instrument was invented by Adolphe Sax in the 1840s. It has a reed in the mouthpiece, which vibrates as air is blown over it. The vibrations create sound waves that resonate the body and bell. As in a flute or oboe, keys change the amount of air which vibrates, and so alter the notes.

9 DRUM

The drum is one of the simplest musical instruments. Yet a good drummer can obtain varied sounds by altering the tension (tightness) of the drum head, hitting it in different places, and using various strikers such as ordinary drum sticks, wire or bristle brushes, or felt-padded hammer-head sticks.

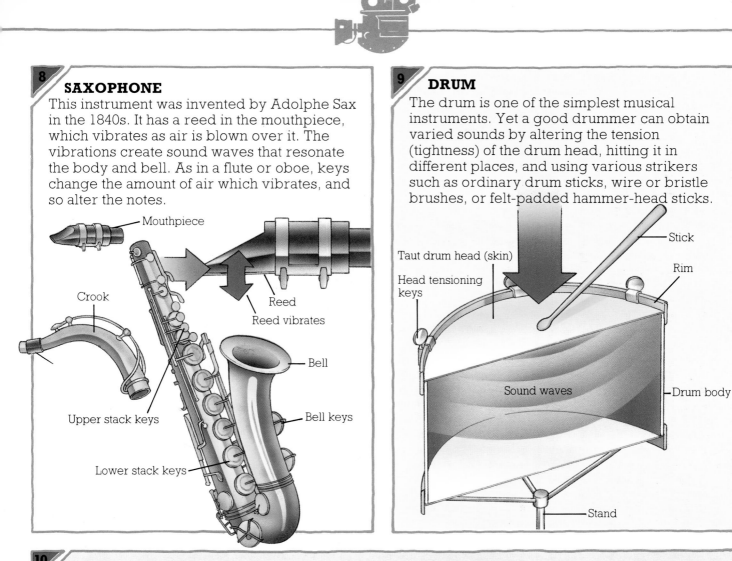

10 ELECTRIC GUITAR

A guitar is a stringed instrument that works in the same basic way as a violin. The string vibrates to give a note according to its length. As the fingers press just behind the frets, shortening the vibrating part of the string, the note becomes higher. In an acoustic guitar, the strings produce sound waves which are amplified by the resonating guitar body.

In an electric guitar, the metal strings vibrate in the magnetic field of the pick-ups. The vibrations alter the amounts of electricity in the wire coils of the pick-ups, creating electrical signals that travel along the lead to the amplifier.

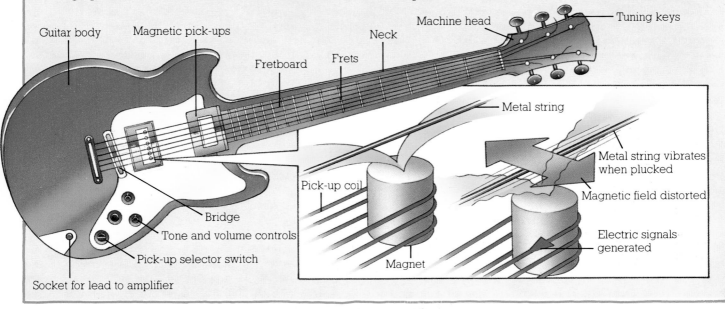

THE FILM SET

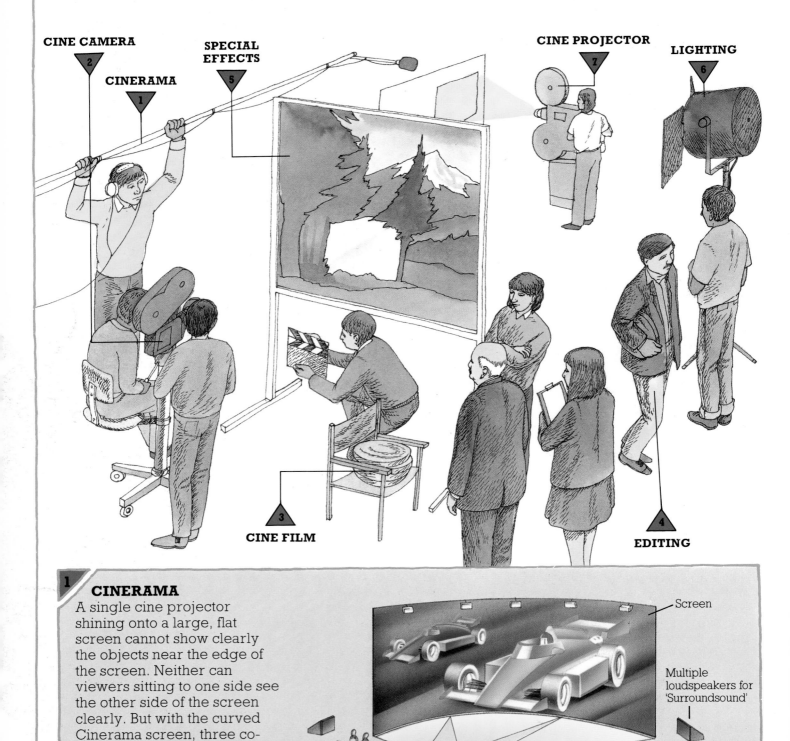

CINE CAMERA

2

CINERAMA

1

SPECIAL EFFECTS

5

CINE PROJECTOR

7

LIGHTING

6

CINE FILM

3

EDITING

4

1

CINERAMA

A single cine projector shining onto a large, flat screen cannot show clearly the objects near the edge of the screen. Neither can viewers sitting to one side see the other side of the screen clearly. But with the curved Cinerama screen, three co-ordinated cameras show different parts of the scene at exactly the same time and the picture 'wraps around' the viewer.

Screen

Multiple loudspeakers for 'Surroundsound'

Three synchronized 35mm projectors

Object

Curved screen

Image at improved angle on curved screen

Viewer

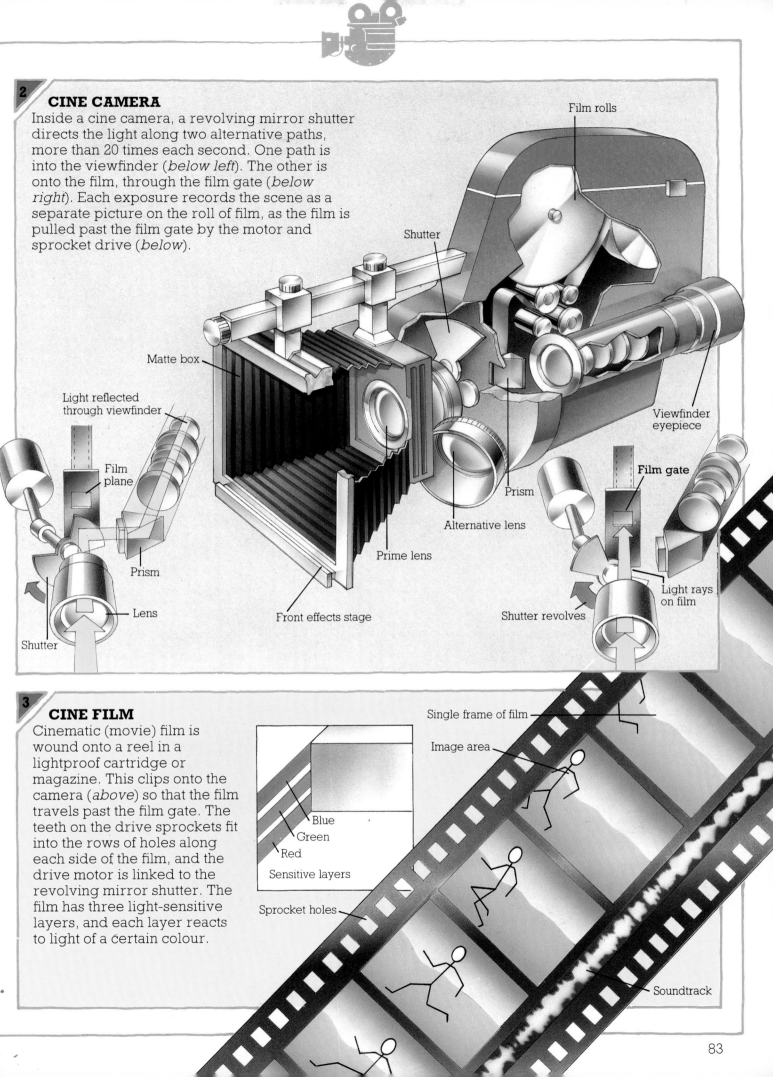

2 CINE CAMERA

Inside a cine camera, a revolving mirror shutter directs the light along two alternative paths, more than 20 times each second. One path is into the viewfinder (*below left*). The other is onto the film, through the film gate (*below right*). Each exposure records the scene as a separate picture on the roll of film, as the film is pulled past the film gate by the motor and sprocket drive (*below*).

Film rolls

Shutter

Light reflected through viewfinder

Film plane

Prism

Lens

Shutter

Matte box

Front effects stage

Prime lens

Alternative lens

Prism

Viewfinder eyepiece

Film gate

Light rays on film

Shutter revolves

3 CINE FILM

Cinematic (movie) film is wound onto a reel in a lightproof cartridge or magazine. This clips onto the camera (*above*) so that the film travels past the film gate. The teeth on the drive sprockets fit into the rows of holes along each side of the film, and the drive motor is linked to the revolving mirror shutter. The film has three light-sensitive layers, and each layer reacts to light of a certain colour.

Blue

Green

Red

Sensitive layers

Sprocket holes

Single frame of film

Image area

Soundtrack

4 EDITING

Few movies are recorded from start to finish on one film roll, in one camera. When editing, the film-maker chooses which individual pictures, or frames, of film should follow each other. The frames are cut up and joined together ('spliced') into the new sequence using glue.

Unwanted frame identified

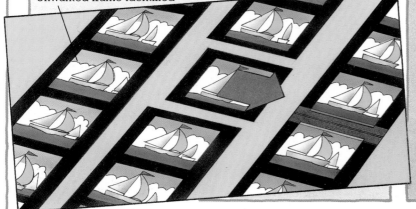

5 SPECIAL EFFECTS

Film-makers use many kinds of special effects to create scenes that do not exist in real life. One method is to film people through a hole in a fake 'background' of painted scenery, called a matte. The people might look as though they are in a huge restaurant, whereas in fact they are at one table, and the rest of the view is painted onto the matte. Another method is to film a person against a blue background, using either camera filters or film that cannot record the blue colour. Another camera records a different background. The two views are blended together before being shown to the viewer. Television weather reports use this technique, but now the weather maps are often created by computer instead of a camera.

6 LIGHTING

There are many different kinds of light sources, such as the fluorescent tube (page 11) and the laser (page 79).

The light bulb is also called the incandescent lamp. It is made of a thin coil of special resistance wire containing the metal tungsten, which can withstand very high temperatures. The wire glows brightly, at a temperature of more than 2500°C, when electricity flows along

it. A special gas mixture inside the glass, or a vacuum of no gas at all, prevents the wire from burning out too quickly. Very powerful incandescent lamps are used to light film sets, so that the cameras can pick up all the details of the actors, objects and scenery. These lamps are rated at many thousands of watts of electricity, compared to the typical home light bulb of about 60, 100 or 150 watts.

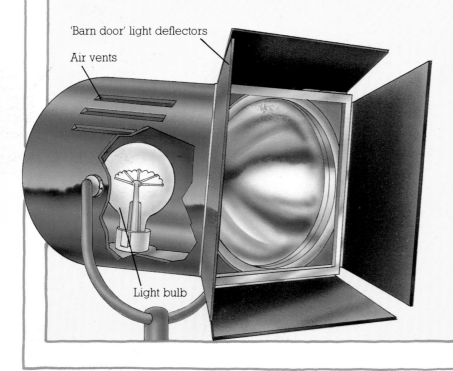

'Barn door' light deflectors

Air vents

Light bulb

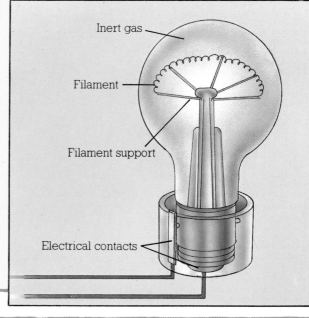

INCANDESCENT LIGHT BULB

Inert gas

Filament

Filament support

Electrical contacts

Scenery painted on matte

Actors

Background

Presenter

Blue screen

Glass matte screen

Weather map

Key area

Camera 1

Camera 2

Viewer sees composite image

Blending box

CINEMA PROJECTOR

The source of light in a typical cinema projector is a powerful xenon lamp. The lamp is so hot that cooling air has to be circulated around it to protect the lamp and the film. The light shines through the film in the film guide, then through a system of lenses and across the cinema onto the screen. The soundtrack is picked up either by an optical reader, if it was recorded in the form of light patterns, or by a magnetic pick-up if it was recorded on magnetic tape.

Film spool

Projection lens

Xenon lamp

Sprockets

Sound drum

Loudspeaker

Amplifier

THEME PARK

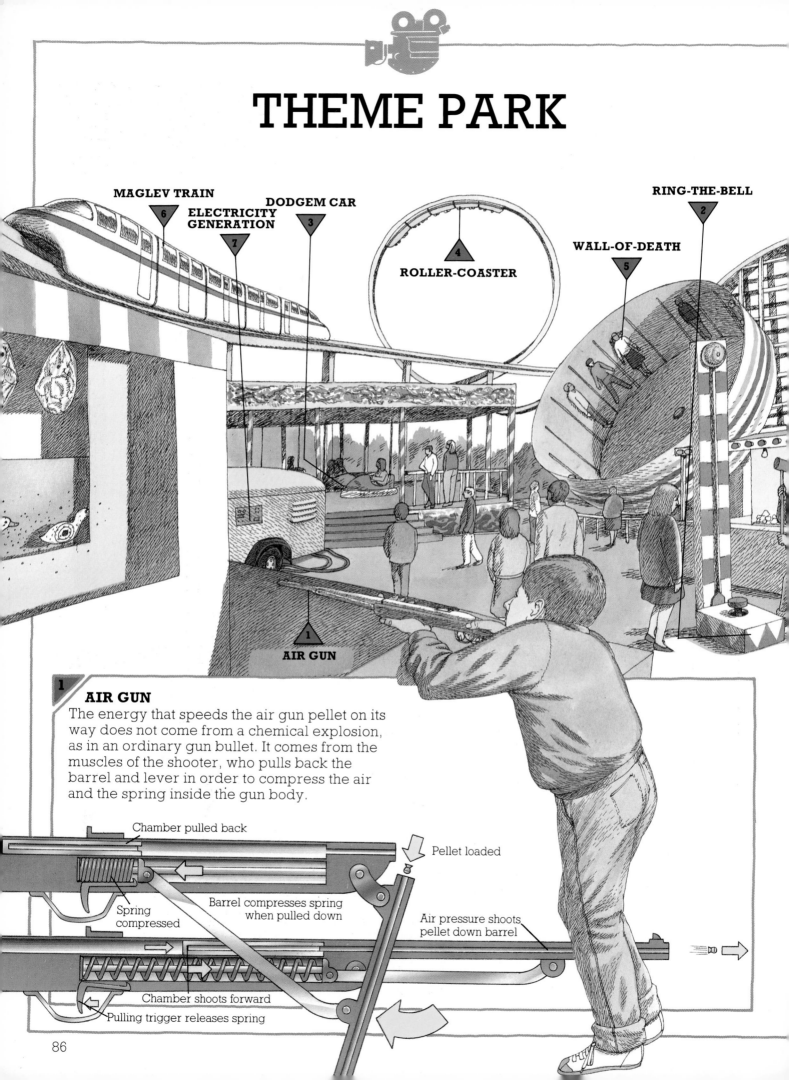

MAGLEV TRAIN 6

ELECTRICITY GENERATION 7

DODGEM CAR 3

ROLLER-COASTER 4

RING-THE-BELL 2

WALL-OF-DEATH 5

AIR GUN 1

1

AIR GUN

The energy that speeds the air gun pellet on its way does not come from a chemical explosion, as in an ordinary gun bullet. It comes from the muscles of the shooter, who pulls back the barrel and lever in order to compress the air and the spring inside the gun body.

Chamber pulled back

Pellet loaded

Spring compressed

Barrel compresses spring when pulled down

Air pressure shoots pellet down barrel

Chamber shoots forward

Pulling trigger releases spring

2 RING-THE-BELL

Like the air gun (*opposite*), energy to work this device comes from the competitor's muscles. A simple lever combines with the physical principle that every action has a reaction (page 73). The hammer crashes down on one end of the lever, lifting the other end, which knocks the clapper upwards. Friction and the force of gravity between the clapper and the rail quickly slow the clapper, so that most hits do not ring the bell at the top.

Rail

5

4

Score scale

3

2

1

Clapper

Hammer

Strike peg

Lever

3 DODGEM CAR

The sliding contact, contact arm, car motor and metal front wheel form part of an electrical circuit, between the metal screen in the roof and the metal floor of the dodgem rink. People standing on the floor are too far away from the roof screen to be in danger of completing the circuit themselves – and being electrocuted. The motor is mounted on the front wheel to avoid the need for complex gears as in a car (page 65). As the dodgem car moves, the sliding contact rubs along the roof screen. Sparks fly between the contact and screen when there are small gaps.

Sliding contact

Metal screen

Contact arm carries electricity from metal screen to car

Steering wheel

½ hp electric motor drives front wheel

Drive belt

All-round bumper

Rubber rear wheels

Metal front wheel carries electricity from car to metal floor

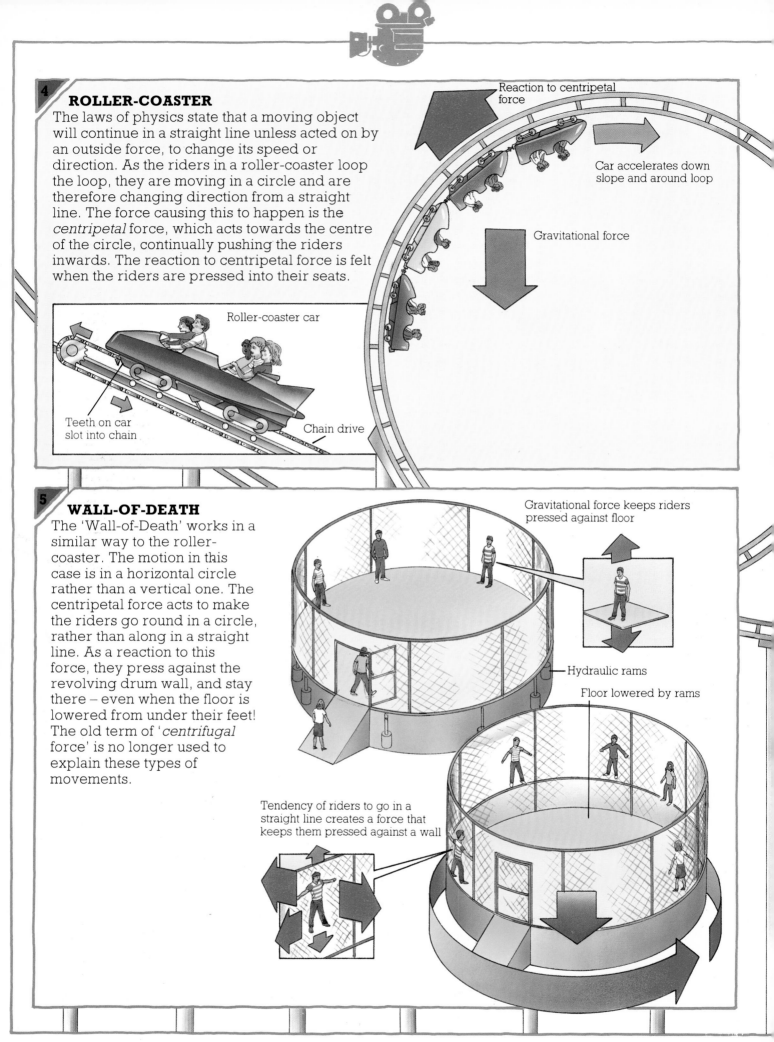

4

ROLLER-COASTER

The laws of physics state that a moving object will continue in a straight line unless acted on by an outside force, to change its speed or direction. As the riders in a roller-coaster loop the loop, they are moving in a circle and are therefore changing direction from a straight line. The force causing this to happen is the *centripetal* force, which acts towards the centre of the circle, continually pushing the riders inwards. The reaction to centripetal force is felt when the riders are pressed into their seats.

Reaction to centripetal force

Car accelerates down slope and around loop

Gravitational force

Roller-coaster car

Teeth on car slot into chain

Chain drive

5

WALL-OF-DEATH

The 'Wall-of-Death' works in a similar way to the roller-coaster. The motion in this case is in a horizontal circle rather than a vertical one. The centripetal force acts to make the riders go round in a circle, rather than along in a straight line. As a reaction to this force, they press against the revolving drum wall, and stay there – even when the floor is lowered from under their feet! The old term of '*centrifugal* force' is no longer used to explain these types of movements.

Gravitational force keeps riders pressed against floor

Hydraulic rams

Floor lowered by rams

Tendency of riders to go in a straight line creates a force that keeps them pressed against a wall

6 MAGLEV TRAIN

A magnet has two poles, North and South. Like poles repel (push apart). Unlike poles attract (pull together). The Maglev train uses this principle. Electromagnets in the train base and the single rail create very powerful magnetic fields. Their poles are arranged so that the train and rail repel each other. The upper repelling force lifts, or levitates, the train so it runs in 'mid-air'. The lower repelling force keeps the train steady as it travels along.

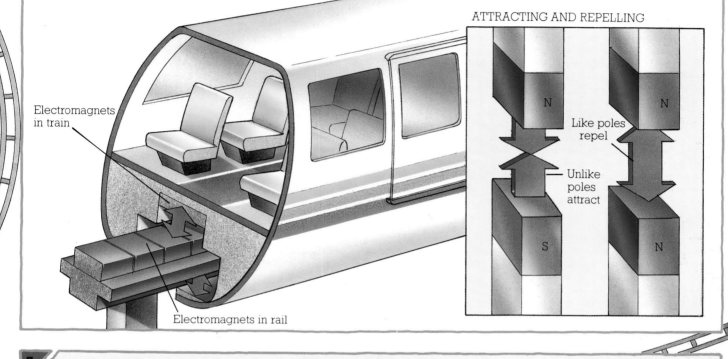

Electromagnets in train

Electromagnets in rail

ATTRACTING AND REPELLING

Like poles repel

Unlike poles attract

7 ELECTRICITY GENERATION

When a wire moves in a magnetic field, an electric current is induced (page 83) in the wire. In the direct-current (DC) generator, wire coils spin between two strong permanent magnets. The electricity induced in the coils reverses its direction as each part of the coil moves from the North to South poles of the magnets, but gaps in the *commutator* mean that a steady direct current is produced. In the alternating-current (AC) generator, each end of the wire coil has a separate brush, so that the current reverses – alternates – with each turn.

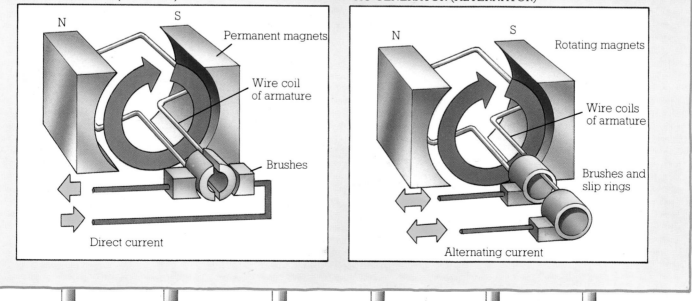

DC GENERATOR (DYNAMO)

N   S

Permanent magnets

Wire coil of armature

Brushes

Direct current

AC GENERATOR (ALTERNATOR)

N   S

Rotating magnets

Wire coils of armature

Brushes and slip rings

Alternating current

GLOSSARY

Aerofoil The specially curved shape of an aircraft wing, when viewed from the side, that produces lift as air flows past it.

Amp (ampere) A unit of measurement for electrical current – the rate of flow of electricity (see also Volt, Watt).

Amplifier An electronic device that makes an electrical signal more powerful or stronger.

Archimedes screw

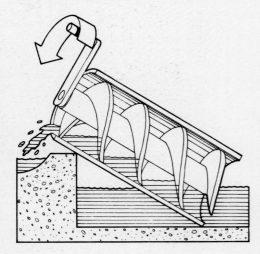

Archimedes screw A long ramp wrapped around a central shaft, like a corkscrew. As it turns it pushes material along its length.

Balance When an object is supported at, or below its centre of gravity, so that gravity does not pull more on one side and tip it over.

Barometer An instrument for measuring air pressure, used in meteorology and in some types of altimeter in aircraft.

Battery The common name for an electrical cell, which makes electricity by chemical reactions. A true 'battery' is really a number of cells joined together.

Bevel gears Gear wheels whose teeth are sloping or at an angle, rather than at right angles to the wheel's flat surface.

Bimetallic strip Two pieces of metal joined so that they bend with changes in temperature, because the two metals expand at different rates.

Bulb A light bulb is a hollow glass globe containing a wire filament, that glows brightly as electricity passes through it.

Cam A 'lump' on an axle or shaft. As it rotates, the cam presses on or moves another part of the machine.

Camber The 'slope' or 'banking' on an object. A cambered road surface allows the rain to drain away and gives better cornering on bends.

Cantilever Part of a structure, such as a bridge, that projects outwards from its support as an 'overhang', and so helps to support the structure.

Centre of gravity The point at which all an object's weight can be thought to be concentrated, so that it balances if supported below this point.

Centrifugal force A force which is often thought to act on an object going in a circle.

Centripetal force The force that keeps an object moving in a circle. Twirl a ball on a string and the 'pull' in the string represents the centripetal force.

Chrominance The part of a television signal that controls the relative brightness of the three colours: red, green and blue.

Circuit In electricity, a series of conductors joined into a loop, around which the electricity flows.

Conductor A substance that allows electricity to pass through it easily. Most metals are good conductors (see also Resistance).

Condenser A device for condensing a substance, changing it from gas to liquid.

Cam

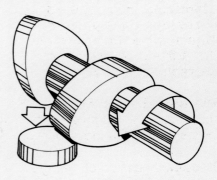

Crank and crankshaft A device for changing a rotary (turning) motion to an oscillating (to-and-fro) one, or vice versa. The shaft has one or more bars, called cranks, fixed to it at an angle. These are usually linked to other bars by pivots. As the shaft turns round, the ends of the bars travel backwards and forwards (see also Oscillation).

Diaphragm A disc or sheet of flexible material which, for example, bends to operate a valve or suck in a fluid.

Drill

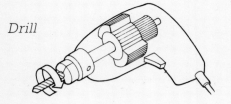

Drill A length of hard material (the drill bit) such as steel, with a sharpened end, turned by a machine such as an electric motor. It gouges out a circular hole as it twists around.

Electricity A type of energy involving electrons or similar particles with an electrical charge. In an electrical circuit, electrons flow from the negative terminal of the battery to the positive one (see Electron).

Electric motor A machine that changes electrical energy into the energy of spinning motion.

Electromagnet A magnet which is magnetized only when electricity passes through the wire coil around it.

Electrostatic When electrical charges are at rest, on or in an object, rather than flowing through a wire as an electric current.

Element (heater) Special wire that resists the flow of electricity, becoming hot in the process.

Escapement In a clock, the mechanism that allows the stored energy in the spring to 'escape' in small, regular amounts.

Feedback Information coming back into a system about the way it is changing. A thermostat, that shuts down the central heating system when the temperature rises above a certain level, is one example (see Thermostat).

Filter A fine net, meshwork or similar material that removes solid impurities from a fluid, or separates larger particles from smaller ones.

Foundations The secure and stable base to a structure, such as a skyscraper or bridge, that stops it sinking into the earth or toppling over.

Four stroke An internal combustion engine driven by pistons that have a complete power cycle every four strokes: down, up, down, up.

Friction When two surfaces 'rub' together as they move past each other. It often produces heat, and can be minimized by lubricating oil.

Fulcrum The pivot point of a lever.

Gear A wheel with V-shaped teeth, cogs or notches around its edge, which meshes with a similar wheel or interlocks with the row of holes in a chain.

Generator A machine that produces electricity from another form of energy, such as moving water (hydroelectricity) or the chemical energy in a fuel like petrol.

Gravity The force of attraction between objects. Usually used for the attraction of the Earth on objects near its surface, pulling them down towards its centre.

Gyroscope A spinning wheel with a heavy rim, on a set of pivots, which tends to resist change in position (see Inertia).

Heat-exchanger A device for transferring heat from one substance to another, for example, when hot exhaust gases pre-warm the cool air coming into an engine.

Hydraulics In a hydraulic machine, fluid – usually special hydraulic oil – is used to transmit pressure along pipes from one part to another.

Hydrophone A type of microphone designed to pick up sounds under water.

Inductance When a magnetic field and nearby conducting wire move relative to each other, creating an electric current in the wire.

Inertia The tendency of objects to stay still or keep moving as they are, resisting any change in position or motion.

Internal combustion engine A machine that changes the chemical energy in fuel, such as petrol, into the energy of a turning shaft, by small 'explosions' (combustions) in an enclosed space, the cylinder.

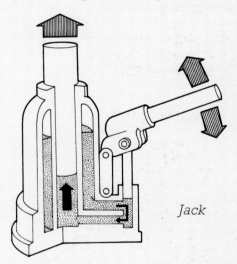

Jack

Jack A lifting machine that raises a heavy load by small amounts, using a smaller effort to move a much greater total distance.

Jet A fast-moving stream of fluid, such as water or air. A jet engine produces a fast-moving stream of hot gases from its exhaust.

Key A specially-shaped object that fits into and opens a lock.

Laser A device that produces a powerful pure-colour beam of light from a gas or crystal, by the process of **L**ight **A**mplification by the **S**timulated **E**mission of **R**adiation.

Lens A specially shaped piece of glass, usually with curved surfaces, that brings light rays together (convergence) or spreads them apart (divergence).

Lever In its simplest form, a rigid bar that pivots on its fulcrum or 'hinge'. Press down on one side, and the other side moves up.

Light A form of energy, as electromagnetic waves, that we can see with our eyes.

Luminance The part of a television signal which controls the overall brightness of the image.

Magnet A piece of material, usually iron-based metal, that has a magnetic field around it and can attract or repel other magnets (see also Electromagnet).

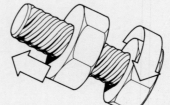

Magnet

Magnetic field Lines of magnetic force around a magnet, that tend to attract or repel other magnets and attract magnetic objects (see also Inductance).

Matte A frame or border used to blank out part of a scene or show scenery, when making films or TV programmes.

Nut In engineering, a flat-sided object with a helical groove in a hole in its centre, that is twisted onto a bolt.

Oscillation Moving to-and-fro or backwards-and-forwards.

Pinion A small gearwheel that meshes with a larger one (see also Rack).

Piston A (usually) cylindrical object that moves up and down inside a hollow cylinder, as in a car engine.

Polarization When the up-and-down motions of waves all happen in the same direction. Without polarization, the ups and downs occur at any angle (sideways, diagonally and so on).

Pressure The force acting on a certain area. The same total force pressing on a surface of 10 square metres, would have 10 times the pressure if it pressed on one square metre.

Primary colours A set of three colours from which all other colours of the spectrum can be obtained, by mixing. For light rays they are usually red, green and blue. For printing inks they are yellow, magenta and cyan.

Prism A piece of transparent material, usually glass or clear plastic, that changes the direction of light rays by reflection or refraction. Some prisms are used to separate white light into the different colours of the spectrum.

Program The sequence of instructions inside a computer, that tell it what to do with the information fed in.

Propellor Angled blades on a central shaft, that 'screw' through a gas or liquid and propel themselves along.

Nut

Quartz crystal A crystal made of quartz (silicon dioxide), which vibrates at a certain frequency when electricity passes through it. The vibrations can be used to control an electronic time-keeping circuit.

Radar RAdio **D**etection **A**nd **R**anging. Navigation or detecting objects using radio waves and/or their reflections (see also Sonar).

Rack and pinion The rack is a row of teeth on a bar, that mesh with the teeth on a pinion (small gear wheel). As the pinion turns, the bar slides along.

Ratchet A point on a bar that presses against sloped teeth on a wheel. The wheel can turn one way, when the 'ramp' on each tooth lifts the point, but the point jams against the teeth and stops the wheel from turning the other way.

Receiver A device that detects waves or signals, such as a radio receiver that picks up radio waves.

Rectifier A device that allows electricity to pass in one direction only. It converts alternating current to direct current.

Reflection When rays 'bounce off' an object, as when light rays reflect from a mirror or sound waves bounce off a wall to give an echo.

Refraction When rays of light bend at the place where they go from one substance into another, such as from air into the glass of a lens.

Resistance When a material resists the flow of electricity. Electrical insulators such as plastics, for example, have very high resistance (see also Conductor).

Resonance When an object vibrates at its own natural frequency, as when a wineglass vibrates and eventually shatters from the sound waves of a certain musical note.

Satellite An object that goes around (orbits) another, usually larger, object. The Moon is a natural satellite of the Earth. Hundreds of artificial satellites orbit the Earth.

Siphon When a continuous stream of fluid flows around an upside-down U tube from a higher level to a lower level. Fluid that is in the down tube 'pulls' more fluid up and around the U bend.

Sonar SOund and **NA**vigation **R**anging. Navigating or detecting objects using sound waves and/or their reflections (see also Radar).

Sound waves Patterns of vibrating molecules which travel through the air, and which we hear as sounds.

Spindle A thin central axle or shaft in a wheel, bobbin, etc.

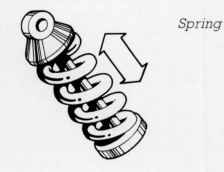

Spring

Spring A coiled device, usually made of metal or special plastic. It can be squeezed or stretched, but always tries to return to its normal length.

Suspension bridge A bridge in which the deck hangs (is suspended from) main cables strung between supporting towers.

Switch A device that opens or closes a gap in an electrical circuit, to stop the electricity or allow it to flow.

Theodolite An instrument that is used by surveyors to measure angles and calculate distances.

Thermostat A 'switch' that turns on or off a heating or cooling system, to keep the temperature roughly constant.

Thrust A propelling force, as when hot gases rush from the back of a jet engine and cause the engine to react by being pushed forwards.

Torque When a force acts in a circular direction, to turn or twist.

Transformer An electrical device that increases or decreases the voltage, with a corresponding fall or rise in the electrical current (see also Amp, Volt).

Transmitter A device that sends out waves or signals, such as a radio transmitter that emits radio waves.

Turbine Angled blades mounted on a central shaft, like a fan. Fluid (such as water or hot gases) moving past the blades makes them spin.

Turbofan A type of jet engine that has a very large fan-like turbine at the front.

Two-stroke An internal combustion engine driven by pistons that have a complete power cycle every two strokes: up, down.

Universal joint Two U-shaped joints pivoted together so that one shaft can transmit its turning motion to another shaft which is at an angle to it.

Valve A device that lets a substance flow one way but not the other (non-return valve), or that controls the rate of flow of a substance, such as water or air.

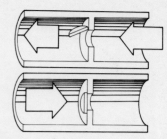

Volt A unit of measurement for the potential difference of electricity, which can be thought of as its 'pushing strength' around the circuit (see also Amp, Watt).

Watt A unit of measurement of power. In an electrical system it is equal to Volts multiplied by Amps (see also Amp, Volt).

Wedge Two sloping ramps placed back-to-back. A wedge forces apart two surfaces when pushed between them.

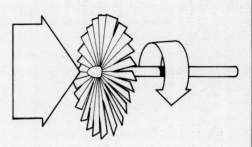

Turbine

Weld A joint made by melting two substances (usually metals), and allowing them to run together before they cool and solidify.

Wheel A disc-shaped object mounted on a central shaft or axle. The wheel is either fixed to the axle or is free to spin on it.

Zip A fastening device in which two rows of teeth-and-sockets are brought together so that they interlock.

INDEX